Developmental
Journey

DEVELOP- MENTAL JOURNEY

A Guide to the Development
of Logical and Moral Reasoning
and Social Perspective

MARY M. WILCOX

ABINGDON  NASHVILLE

DEVELOPMENTAL JOURNEY:

A Guide to the Development of Logical
and Moral Reasoning and Social Perspective

Copyright © 1979 by Abingdon

Library of Congress in Publication Data

WILCOX, MARY M. 1921-
    Developmental journey.
    Bibliography: p.
    Includes index.
1. Reasoning. 2. Decision-making. 3. Thought and
thinking. 4. Education—Philosophy. 5. Developmental
psychology. I. Title.
BC177.W48   153.4   79-1340

ISBN 0-687-10510-2

Book Designer: L. B. Wooten

MANUFACTURED BY THE PARTHENON PRESS AT
NASHVILLE, TENNESSEE, UNITED STATES OF AMERICA

To June and Karrie

PREFACE

This book emerges from two major sources. One is the teaching I have done with two colleagues at the Iliff School of Theology, Dr. Clarence H. Snelling, Professor of Teaching Ministries, and Dr. H. Edward Everding, Associate Professor of New Testament. We have conducted many courses and workshops for public school teachers, teachers of religion, graduate students, college students, parents, and adolescents. The questions and concerns of these students and participants are reflected in the content and style of this book.

The second source is a research project which H. Edward Everding and I conducted in 1975. This project has provided most of the dialogue quoted from interviews as well as the data in the area of social perspective which together constitute a major emphasis in this book. With its roots in both research and student responses, the book strives to be an effective blend of the theoretical and the practical.

Individuals who have contributed significantly to the content of the book are: the scorers in the 1975 research project, Suzanne Calvin, Barbara N. Hays, Carol MacEachern, Lois J. Shugart, and Mary Elva Smith; the student teaching interns at the Iliff School of Theology, Monte J. Baker, JoAnn G. Brekke, Anna Jo Eads, Sandra V. Edwards, Carole MacEachern, Robert L. Oram, Robert J. Rohdenburg, Mary Elva Smith, Patricia L. Vick, Gary L. Whetstone, Kathie R. Wilson, and James S. Whitt, whose part in shaping the way the material is presented in courses is reflected in the organization of the book; the people who critiqued earlier forms of the manuscript, Suzanne Calvin, Vasiliki Eckley, David T. Hartman, Dean

C. Hirt, Margaret R. Hirt, and Mary Elva Smith; my husband Ray, who has been my major critic and support, always ready with questions about overuse of technical jargon, and willing to spend vacations with a wife with a typewriter; and the many persons who contributed their time and mental effort to the interviews that are the basis of this book (guarantees of confidentiality require that these individuals remain anonymous).

Finally, I want to express appreciation to the Iliff School of Theology which has provided the setting for the research and for much of the teaching and generation of creative ideas.

Mary M. Wilcox
May 1978

CONTENTS

Developmental
Journey

CHAPTER I
Introduction

IS IT ALL RIGHT TO BREAK THE LAW?

Janie answered this question: "No, you get in trouble. . . . But it's all right if you're the boss, you won't get in trouble."

Herbert Porter, a Watergate participant, answered the question in a different way as he explained his part in illegal actions. "Well . . . my loyalty to one man, Richard Nixon . . . I felt I had known this man all my life . . . not personally, perhaps, but in spirit. I felt a deep sense of loyalty. I was appealed to on this basis."[1]

And Egil Krogh, who authorized the break-in of the office of Daniel Ellsberg's psychiatrist, reflected on his actions at the time of his sentencing in a different way. "But however national security is defined, I now see that none of the potential uses of the sought information could justify the invasion of the rights of the individuals that the break-in necessitated. The understanding I have come to is that these rights are the definition of our nation. . . ."[2]

These quotations are examples of different ways in which people reason when they make decisions about right and wrong. And this book is about people: Janie and other children . . . public figures like Porter and Krogh . . . real youth and adults who could well be you and me or our friends, business associates, teachers, or students. It explores how we understand decision-making, why we often disagree about important issues, and how we can facilitate better communication and understanding. It describes how all of us learn to consider "right and wrong" in progressively more complex ways. It really tells about the journey of the human mind as it functions for us to make sense and meaning of our world.

Let's continue by listening to a group of high school students who are discussing a moral dilemma:

"Should a man have the right, morally and legally, to steal an overpriced drug for which he cannot pay, in order to save his dying wife?"

The question has just been asked: "Is it all right to break the law?"

One student replies, "Well, it depends on if you are a good person or a bad person, and maybe on how much you love your wife."

Another disagrees, "No, that doesn't have anything to do with it. What if everybody thought they could break the law? I can see the man's point, but stealing is against the law, it's illegal."

Other students join in.

"I think it depends on how much the man needs his wife. If he doesn't like her, why risk getting thrown in jail? Let her die, and then get another wife."

"You shouldn't do it. You'll get thrown in jail for the robbery."

"If laws are unfair, you should have a court. Try to change them. If it's a hard decision, they'll go through the higher courts. But you shouldn't just break the law."

"I think in this case it would be all right because we are all God's children, and I believe we should have responsibility for the whole human race. Besides, it was his wife and she should be his responsibility."[3]

Note the variety of reasons given by these students, both for and against breaking the law. They include some of the same kinds of reasons given by Janie, Porter, and Krogh. In each of the quotations, which are statements by real people, we are hearing how individuals struggle with moral issues. We, as readers, may prefer some reasons over others, and we may be impatient to step into the discussion with our own ideas. I hope that this book will be a dialogue between the reader and other human minds as they struggle with making sense and "right" decisions in a world of conflicting information and commitments.

Introduction

We are living in a time when relativism is the norm, when many old standards seem inadequate in the face of complicated questions and situations, when major issues confront us daily.

The energy crisis presents a myriad of seemingly unsolvable problems:

—the need for more and more energy versus reduction and conservation in the future

—stripping of the land versus environmental concerns

—conflicting information about the use of nuclear power

—Where do you place priorities? How do restrictions and laws affect, not only you, but other persons in radically different situations?

Abortion is a legal, medical, religious, political, and ethical issue of staggering proportions. Medical advances raise new questions:

—How does one decide about maintaining or withdrawing life support systems from a dying relative? Does the age of that relative make a difference?

—How does a medical transplant team make the decision of whether to use an available kidney for an older man or for a young ex-heroin addict?

The Mylai incident of the Vietnam War raised serious questions about the consequences of blind obedience to authority. Unethical behavior in the political realm has come under critical scrutiny by a disturbed press and citizenry. Issues related to capital punishment and equal rights are of continuing concern to voters. More permissive sexual attitudes and new forms of life-style offer bewildering alternatives.

Educators and educational institutions, both secular and religious, are making a variety of responses to this urgent interest in values and the process of decision-making. Two traditional views taken by educators in regard to the teaching of values are:

First, it is not the business of the schools to teach people what their values should be. That should be left to the home and the church.

Second, schools should teach the traditional values upon which everyone agrees.

Recently, a third view has become popular: values are relative, and the important thing is to help each person know what his or her own values are. It is not the responsibility of the school to judge these values in any way; let each student decide which values to appropriate. Many public schools and religious institutions have rejected the first two views and appear to be choosing this third approach, implemented through a process called "values clarification."

The intent of this book is to draw attention to another option: the process of valuing and making decisions approached in the light of gradual growth and development. People make decisions according to different criteria, as illustrated in the classroom discussion and quotations listed earlier. But when their reasons for decisions are examined, there is an amazing similarity in the patterns through which each child, youth, and adult progresses. In this book my purposes are:

(1) to describe the developmental journey taken by persons in their thinking about the physical world, about persons and society, about moral issues, and about symbols,

(2) to suggest an educational model that builds on and enhances the development of such thinking and perceiving, as well as feeling,

(3) to describe ways of implementing the model through the use of values clarification, moral and social dilemmas, and other strategies,

(4) to organize and clarify without oversimplifying, and

(5) to direct the reader toward other resources which amplify points that cannot be thoroughly dealt with in this book.

The presentation of this subject matter is aimed

primarily at a general audience of educators, college and graduate students, and parents. The final chapter suggests application of this material in a religious setting.

DEVELOPMENTAL JOURNEY: THE THEORIES OF PIAGET AND KOHLBERG

An infant's legs are chubby, bowed, short, and kick aimlessly, and the feet curve in. It is no wonder that he/she is unable to walk or run. By contrast, the legs of the track star are long, muscular, and function with beautiful coordination. Both pairs of legs are composed of the same parts: feet, ankles, calves, knees, and thighs. But what a difference in structure; how much more complex and efficient are the legs of the track star. No amount of training and practice will produce such skill in the baby. We take this kind of change for granted in the parts of the physical body as the baby grows through childhood and adolescence and finally into adulthood. The adult is more than a big child. Mature physical structure allows for complex kinds of functioning that are impossible for the child at earlier stages. Yet each new stage grows from and includes previous stages, and there is no return. Physical bodies may deteriorate, but they never regress to the less efficient and simpler structure of earlier stages.

There are other kinds of structural changes in a person which are not so readily observable as the physical ones. Recent research shows that the development of logical, social, and moral reasoning is directly related to structural changes in the way the mind operates. This can be illustrated in a stylized diagram representing patterns formed by the nervous and sensory systems. In a new baby this pattern is simple, so simple that it can be represented by a set of squares which relate to the baby's sucking ability (figure 1a). As the baby learns to grasp, another little set of structures appears which we can represent by circles (figure 1b). The circles are not connected to the squares because at first the baby cannot coordinate sucking and grasping.

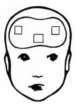

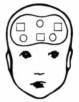

Figure 1a   Figure 1b

But gradually the baby learns to reach for an object and grasps it in order to suck it. During this interaction between the physical activity of the body and the mental processing of the brain, two sets of activities and two sets of structures become coordinated and connected. In this way a new structure is formed (figure 2).

In a similar way, the small infant watches his or her feet overhead, kicking in the air, a fascinating and unexplained activity. Gradually he/she discovers that those objects can be controlled and made to do interesting things. This is the beginning of the realization that: "Those are *my* feet. I am separate from my environment, I am one object and there are other objects." The infant is sorting out a few items from a big undifferentiated mass of things and actions.

He or she is organizing the world. The child is not memorizing a fact, but is beginning to set up and internalize a basic way of looking at the self and the world. We don't "forget" this new organization, as we may forget the names of even close acquaintances, because it is more than a simple addition of information to be stored in the mind. The addition of information, represented by putting Xs inside the structures (figure 3) is important, but it is not the same process as developing the internal structure that determines the manner in which the mind handles, or operates upon, information.

The structure filters out, is unable to accept, all information which is too dissimilar from its "shape." It may be compared with the keyhole which accepts only what already fits—a particular key—or something that

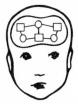 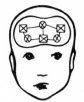

Figure 2   Figure 3

can be molded to its shape. In a similar way, the lenses in a pair of glasses shape what the wearer sees in the surrounding world. Thus, the structure or keyhole of the mind rejects or shapes incoming information.

For example, if a baby is asked to add 2 + 2, there is too much disparity between this external stimulus and the pattern or structure in the baby's mind. The mind can't "compute," and the stimulus bounces off. But if confronted by a concrete object, even pieces of dirt and old cigarette butts, the child's mind can change these to sucking objects. As adults, we may consider this a radical distortion of reality, but this common example demonstrates real interaction between an infant and its environment. And development in thinking comes as a result of such interactions between the innate structure of the mind and the materials and activities of the environment.

The example above suggests why we cannot force the baby to talk, or do arithmetic, before the brain can handle the activity, any more than we can force the baby to walk before the body structure is ready. Structural change cannot be hastened significantly beyond its natural time clock, nor apparently can steps in the maturing process be skipped. However, the process can be and often is prematurely slowed or stopped. Furthermore, there is some indication that pressuring a child with stimuli before the mind is ready may create a prejudice against that type of information in the future. This may inhibit learning at a later time when the young person might otherwise have been ready and enthusiastic about the subject matter.

The process of structural development, described in more detail in the following chapters, is based primarily on the research of two men, Jean Piaget and Lawrence Kohlberg. Piaget, a Swiss scientist, spent many years recording the development of children from birth through puberty, beginning with his own children in infancy. Originally trained as a biologist, Piaget built his theory of development on genetic or hereditary factors. However, he did not assume that the developmental process was strictly physical—to be viewed in the same way as the inevitable maturational development of plants and lower forms of animal life. Neither did he assume that learning was primarily a matter of social stimulation and reaction. He built a theory based on both genetic factors and social interaction. He made observations of infants and children as they interacted with certain situations and noted the progress they made in mastering various tasks. From these observations he worked out a detailed description of the patterns used by infants and children in relating to physical objects and actions in the environment. He found that all children seemed to take the same journey, that is, to follow the same sequence, although some journeyed more quickly than others. He discovered that in this process there were several distinguishable milestones, and he divides the sequence into what he calls "periods" and "stages." The development of logical structures described in the following chapters is based primarily on Piaget's description of the sequence and is supported by examples derived from my own interviews and those of co-researchers.

Building on the work of Piaget, Lawrence Kohlberg and associates of Harvard's Graduate School of Education, have demonstrated that there is a similar pattern of development in the structures of social perspective (view of people and society) and moral reasoning. Just as Piaget discovered the varying ways in which infants, children, and youth deal with and react to physical objects and actions, so Kohlberg found a definite progression in the

20

manner that children, youth, and adults understand and reason about other people and questions of value. His sequence is described as a series of "levels" and "stages," varying in length for different individuals, but following the same developmental journey. The development of social perspective and moral reasoning described in the following chapters is based originally on Kohlberg's work, with significant insights from the research of James W. Fowler, Robert G. Kegan, James R. Rest, and Robert L. Selman. My own work has contributed a new organization for social perspective. Most of the examples are from research that H. Edward Everding and I conducted.[4] A fourth area, the use of symbol, is closely related to the work of Piaget and Kohlberg and comes from the research of James W. Fowler in faith development.

In defining the periods, stages, and levels of development, both Piaget and Kohlberg stress that it is the *structure* of the reasoning process that is changing. The school age child reasons differently from the infant about physical objects, social relationships, values, ideals, and moral questions, and an adult may be expected to think in yet other ways about all such areas of experience. The basis for the change in each instance is the way in which the brain structures, patterns, or organizes data and thinks about experiences. The patterns or stages are seen as broad landmarks on a normal journey through which all persons may travel. Time spent in any one stage, as well as the final stage reached, is different for each individual but the sequence is similar.

The developmental journey is a fluid and fluctuating PROCESS of interaction. The stages represent a series of steps which cannot be retraced and which provide ever more complex understandings of the physical, social, moral and symbolic worlds. Each stage is a new structure, a restructuring of all previous stages. It is a new and expanded way of looking at one's world and involves a liberation from some of the limitations of the previous stage.

21

Both Piaget and Kohlberg affirm that the social environment is the primary stimulus to growth and development. Thus the role of parents, teachers, and others in the social world of the infant, child, maturing youth, or adult becomes crucial in providing contexts which allow for normal development. One of the major purposes of this work is to describe the sequences of growth and to illustrate them in contexts readily available to parents and teachers who in turn may relate them to the growing and developing processes they encounter in the persons with whom they are involved.

THE WHOLE PERSON

We must keep in mind that a person is a very complex entity with physical, intellectual, and emotional components all interacting with one another. But for the purpose of gathering research data, it is most effective to look at one aspect at a time. Some of my students coined the phrase "concentric circle person pie" as a way of describing the different components of a person (figure 4). The person is the whole pie, and we can separate out segments or "pieces" to be looked at individually. The concentric circles represent growth and expansion of each piece as the person journeys through life (figure 5).

Figure 4

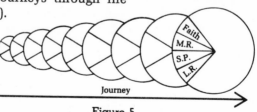

Journey

Figure 5

I want to stress that behavior, emotions, moral and logical thinking, and imagination and intuition are all parts of the same journey. No part can be exchanged for another, nor can a person function effectively without development in each part.[5] The intention of this book is to describe three pieces of the pie in a major way and explore a fourth in a minor way. Then in chapter 8, an educational model is presented that integrates these pieces with other aspects of the whole person. Here are the four points of view:

1. *Logical reasoning,* based on the work of Piaget, describes how a person understands physical reality in terms of making sense of objects, actions, space, time. It appears that logical development is a necessary basis for the development of the second point of view.

2. *Social perspective* concerns how one perceives and interprets persons and society. It is based on the work of James W. Fowler, Lawrence Kohlberg, Robert G. Kegan, James R. Rest, and Robert L. Selman, with additions suggested by my own work. It forms the context for the third point of view.

3. *Moral reasoning* or how one reasons about right and wrong on moral issues, is based primarily on Kohlberg's work.

4. *Role of symbols,* a minor part of this presentation in terms of quantity of material, is a part of the faith development model of James W. Fowler. It deals with how persons use symbols in making meaning out of their lives.

These four "pieces of the pie," shown in figure 6, are grouped under the overarching term "cognitive development," meaning to *know,* and referring to intellectual activities of the mind. This concept is explained more fully in chapter 4.

It is my hope that this book will reveal some new insights on pieces of the pie which have been dimly perceived in the past, and that it will also place these in an integrated perspective. For this purpose, I have arranged

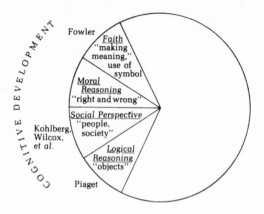

Figure 6

the presentation of developmental structure in broad age divisions so that each period can be viewed somewhat holistically. For each age group, we will be looking at the structure of reasoning from the three major viewpoints with some attention to the fourth. The danger of presenting this material in age divisions is that it tends to give the impression that specific stages are restricted to particular ages. It must be remembered that development does not take place in lockstep fashion within a rigid time schedule. Throughout the descriptions I will be pointing out the flexibility and many variations characteristic of our developmental journeys.

The three major viewpoints are summarized in the foldout chart found at the back of the book. You may find this chart helpful in organizing and summarizing material as you read through the book.

At the end of each chapter there is a short quiz. This is for those readers who are interested in checking with themselves to see if the blank spaces in their minds are filled in with a few new Xs. In other words, is the content of the chapter coming through to you?

QUIZ

Try matching the answers in Column B with the statements in Column A.

Column A	Column B
1. Human development in reasoning is the result of _____	1. values clarification
2. Jean Piaget is responsible for a theory of _____	2. interaction between the innate structure of the mind and the materials and activity of the environment
3. Lawrence Kohlberg has described theories of _____	3. logical development
4. An approach to values education based on the belief that values are relative is commonly called _____	4. varying time intervals
5. People progress through periods, levels, and stages in the same sequence but at _____	5. development of social perspective and moral reasoning
6. The development of one's reasoning structure is not the same as the addition of information but is the _____	6. development of a new way of looking at one's world

ANSWERS

1. 2   2. 3   3. 5   4. 1   5. 4   6. 6

CHAPTER II

Beginning the Journey: The Infant and Small Child

INTRODUCTION

In this chapter we take a look at the infant and small child from the three major viewpoints: logical reasoning, social perspective, and moral reasoning. In order to see the relationship among these three and how they correlate with age, I have represented them in (figure 1). (See foldout chart at the back of the book.)

Viewpoints ("Windows")	Divisions	Periods . . .	Levels/Stages
Moral Reasoning	*Issues* Life Law etc.	Stage 0	**Preconventional Level** Stage 1
Social Perspective	*Factors* Authority Law etc.	Stage 0	**Preconventional Level** Stage 1
Logical Reasoning	*Operations* Conservation Seriation Reversibility etc.	*Sensorimotor Period* Ages 0–1½ (approx.)	*Preoperational Period* Ages 1½–7 (approx.)

Figure 1

The chart shows, first, that logical reasoning is the basis for the other two, that it underlies them. Second, it demonstrates that the child's *Preoperational Period* must precede Stage 1 of social perspective which must precede Stage 1 of moral reasoning. And third, it suggests that ages are only approximate and are significant primarily in logical reasoning.

Divisions within each viewpoint are simply suggested here by their titles and two or three examples: moral reasoning is divided into "issues," social perspective into "factors," and logical reasoning into "operations." The details will be supplied as each viewpoint is considered more thoroughly.

In this chapter we will be looking at the logical reasoning, social perspective, and moral reasoning of infants and young children through about seven years of age.

LOGICAL REASONING:
WAYS OF THINKING ABOUT PHYSICAL OBJECTS

I open this chapter with a brief introduction to Piaget's ideas about the development of logical reasoning in the infant and small child. Piaget's scheme consists of four major periods. The first of these, designated the *Sensorimotor Period*, describes the development of thinking during approximately the first year and a half to two years of life. This is how the human journey starts when we begin to make sense of the concrete world.

The *Preoperational Period* grows out of sensorimotor processes and characterizes the thinking of children during the preschool years—and sometimes beyond. It evolves into the *Period of Concrete Operations*, which begins during the early school years for most children and not uncommonly continues to be the major mode of thinking for youth and adults. This is followed by the *Period of Formal Operations* which may begin in early adolescence. These last two periods will be described in subsequent chapters. All four periods are summarized in the foldout chart.

THE SENSORIMOTOR PERIOD: CRIB LIFE [1]

The development of the brain's structure can be observed in the infant primarily through physical and motor activities and through the ways in which sensory perceptions are handled. The thinking of infants develops directly from the way they handle, feel, taste, smell, and otherwise act on physical objects and from how these objects respond to their actions.

27

An infant experiences him or herself as the center of his/her personal world. We call this egocentrism. As the earth once seemed to ancient people to be the center of the universe with all the heavenly bodies revolving around it, so does the world seem to revolve around each infant. When the digestive tract hurts, the baby cries, the cry produces milk, and the pain disappears. When the little body feels damp and cold, a cry produces a warm, clean, dry feeling. The child IS the universe.

But gradually the infant becomes aware of distinctions. The fascinating hands and feet waving in the air are found to be attached to his/her own body. The rattle or doll is separate from that body. The one who supplies milk is a significant other. This gradual sorting out of the infant's physical world is an amazing process, accomplished within a few months after birth. Certain aspects of such learning can be measured by careful observation of infant responses.

As the infant develops awareness of the physical and social environment, the task of communication with that environment becomes crucial. The infant assumes that all others see the world in exactly the same way as he or she sees it. This may be the source of much infant frustration and anger. When the child meets with opposition, his or her outburst may be as if to say, "Why don't they see what is obvious to ME?" (The effects of such egocentricity in relationships with other people will be described in the next section of this chapter.)

The *Sensorimotor Period* is a time of continuing progress in reasoning about physical objects. Soon after an infant learns to differentiate the self from other objects and persons, another crucial concept appears, that of "object constancy." Lack of object constancy is when a baby drops a bottle or toy, and although the object remains in the crib and the baby is capable of turning over, the infant makes no attempt to look for it. In the early sensorimotor period what cannot be seen ceases to exist. But by the end of the first year the infant discovers that dropped toys have not passed into oblivion. Objects have lives of their own! This fact is tested by repeated dropping of toys and food and peering intently at the fallen object. It is still there! "Peek-a-boo" is another way of experimenting with this exciting new idea of object constancy.

Yet objects not found in expected places are still considered nonexistent. It takes months of testing and experiencing before the small child's structure of thinking makes room for the knowledge that objects have lives of their own, that they exist even when the child has no contact with them.

The overriding intellectual task of the *Sensorimotor Period* is to learn about objects by using or acting upon them. The ways in which humans learn to view their physical world produce the bedrock or basic structure for how all other aspects of life are seen. This is the fundamental keyhole or lens. For instance, the small child's egocentrism and limited understanding of the physical world severely constricts his or her conceptions of people and society. In the small infant, all attachment is centered on the self. As the child tests object constancy, he or she begins to form attachments for those objects which are known, including the person objects that are a part of his/her world.

Imagine watching a slide show, put together without any order, using slides from other people's vacation trips. There would be no logic to it, and many of the objects would be unfamiliar. If we could get inside the world-view of the small child, the events of an ordinary day might appear as just such a series of unrelated and disconnected "pictures." Although the child is not aware of the concept of unrelatedness in adult terms these events and objects would seem strange and without logical connections to inform our understanding. No wonder the child begins to ask, "What's that?" and "Why?"

The *Sensorimotor Period* is summarized in the foldout chart.

THE PREOPERATIONAL PERIOD: THE CHILD OF WONDER [2]

Piaget's *Preoperational Period* describes a kind of thinking common to children between the ages of about one and a half and seven years, although there may be significant variation from these limits. The child's ability to relate to the world has expanded from "learning through physical actions" to the use of language. This new language skill involves the naming of objects and verbal communication about them. At this point, the ability to use language is a critical feature in the child's developmental journey. It is as if each infant were born into a hopelessly tangled jungle. The baby knows only a very small clearing. All he or she learns is in the immediate response to sensorimotor experience; but each new logical advance makes a little more order, a little larger clearing of meaning in the jungle (figure 2). The newly acquired language skill gives us a new insight into development, so in the following descriptions I make extensive use of actual conversations with children.[3]

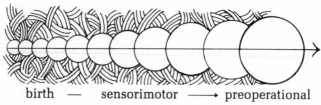

birth — sensorimotor ——→ preoperational

Figure 2

Three-year-old Janie and I sit at a table with two pieces of clay. Here is a record of our conversation.

Interviewer: Janie, what's this?
J: Play dough.
I: What do you do with play dough?
J: Make something out of it.
I: Are you going to make something out of it?
J: Uh huh. Put it down here.

(Janie pats the clay.)

30

I: Can you make your piece into a nice round ball? And I'll make mine into a nice round ball, too . . . Do yours and mine look about the same size?

J: Yes.

I: Do you think they have about the same amount of clay in them?

J: Yes.

I: Now, can you smash one?

(Janie loudly smacks one of the balls and flattens it into a pancake.)

I: You like to do that, don't you? Now, do they still have the same amount?

J: No.

I: Which has more?

(Janie points to the round ball.)

I: Why does that one have more clay?

J: Because this one's smashed. *(Janie points to the pancake.)*

Janie's reply is a typical one for a three-year-old. To her, things are what they appear to be. She depends on immediate perceptions and "centers" on a single striking feature; fixating on the thinness of the pancake, she does not see that it has also greatly increased in diameter. (Some children center on the "fatness" of the ball, perceiving it as more.) Her brain structure has long ago adapted to the concept of object constancy, but "conservation of amount," the recognition that the amount constituting an object remains the same even when its shape changes, may be several years in the future.

Janie and I played another game with seven straws which had been cut into different lengths (figure 3a). Janie was asked to arrange them in order from shortest to longest, side by side—like stair steps. She carefully laid out four of the straws, lining them up at the bottom, but then did not know what to do with the remaining three straws (figure 3b).

31

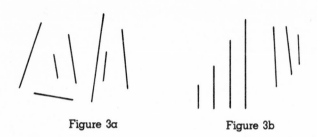

Figure 3a   Figure 3b

This process of arranging objects in a series according to length, size, weight, or any other property, is called "seriation." The preoperational child is able to accomplish this only with a limited number of objects and only by a trial and error approach.

I put three cardboard mountains on a table with a tiny doll, who, I explained to Janie, was taking pictures of the mountains (figure 4).[4]

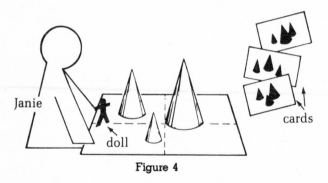

Figure 4

I had a series of cards with drawings of the mountains, "photographs" taken from different points of view. I placed the doll directly in front of Janie and showed her a "picture" the doll had taken from that point of view. Janie agreed that it was the right picture. But when I moved the doll to other positions, she was unable to choose any pictures corresponding to the doll's new perspectives. No matter where the doll was placed, Janie continued to choose the picture which represented HER view.

32

This is an example of egocentrism, which continues into the *Preoperational Period.* It is demonstrated again in an interview with three-year-old Mike who has a brother named Charlie.

Interviewer: Mike, do you have a brother?
Mike: Yes.
I: What is your brother's name?
M: Charlie.
I: Does Charlie have a brother?
M: No . . . yes.
I: What is Charlie's brother's name?
M: Daddy.

Mike knows that he has a brother, but he does not know that he is a brother to Charlie. He does not reverse his thinking, a characteristic called "irreversibility." This means that:

(1) he cannot retrace his steps to look for a misplaced toy, he simply searches at random;

(2) he does not understand that a clay ball can be made into a pancake and then reversed to its original shape without varying its amount;

(3) he cannot put himself in Charlie's place and see himself as a brother to Charlie;

(4) he cannot put himself in the physical place of another person and look at the world from that person's vantage point, as in the case of the doll and the mountains. Even less can he do this in relationship to feelings and other differing points of view. The significance of the logical structure for the other "pieces of the pie" becomes very clear.

Another aspect of egocentrism is that children view the world as created for them personally and believe that they can control it. This belief is manifested in a strong sense of magic. Piaget has given us a delightful quotation from one of his interviews that demonstrates yet another quality of preoperational thinking. This quality, animism, attributes life to inanimate objects. "The moon looks at us and

33

watches over us," says Ga (8½), "when I walk, it walks; when I stand still it stands still. It copies like a parrot."

"Why?"——"It wants to do whatever I do."

"Why?"——"Because it's inquisitive."[5]

Janie tells a charming story about a dream in which a sheep comes into her bedroom and snuggles with her. She concludes, "and in the morning I saw him!" She often cannot distinguish fact from fantasy nor play from reality, as we perceive it, and she finds no need to do so. She explains the source of her ideas as "I dreamed that " or "I just knowed it " or "God told me." Because of the quality of such thinking processes, this period is sometimes labeled Prelogical.

The main task in the development of logic during this period is to learn to represent or think about what has been previously learned from acting on objects during the *Sensorimotor Period*. Here represent means the ability to:

(1) form a mental picture or image of an action or object, thus enabling the child to "recall" it;

(2) imitate the action or object, even when it is not immediately present, called "deferred imitation";

(3) use words (language) to refer to the action or object.

Let us continue the conversation with Janie about the clay balls to perceive the function of mental images and language in the development of logical representation.

After Janie insisted that the smashed ball contained less clay than the round one, I asked:

I: Did you take some clay away from this smashed one?

J: No.

I: But you think it doesn't have as much in it? . . . Can you make it the same again?

J: I'll make this one bigger.

(She makes the pancake into a ball)

I: Are you adding some more clay to it?

J: Uh huh. (Meaning yes)

I: Where'd you get the clay from that you are adding to it?

(Janie spots a small piece of clay lying near me and points to it.)

I: From that one? I didn't see you take any.

(Janie makes the two clay balls into snakes.)

J: Are they the same size?
I: What do you think?
J: They're the same size. Now we smash one.

(Janie smashes one of the snakes.)

I: Now what?
J: Now I think they're different.
I: They look different, don't they? Do you think they have a different amount of clay in them?
J: *(Pointing to the snake)* This one's different because this one isn't smashed.
I: *(Pointing to the smashed snake)* Did you take any clay from this one?
J: Yes.
I: Where did you put the clay you took away?

(Janie points to a small piece lying on the table.)

I: I don't think you did. That was already there. Watch me, Janie. I'm going to smash this one. See if I take any clay away.

(I smash one snake.)

I: Did I take any clay away?
J: No.
I: Okay, now you make one into a snake again. Let's leave this one smashed, like you smashed it . . . Now, is there the same amount of clay in them?
J: No.
I: Did you take any away? Did you put any more in this one?

35

J: Yes.
I: Where did you get it? All you did was roll it.

(Janie points to a piece of clay.)

I: No, I don't think you did.
J: I took it away from here and put it in here.
I: You know what I think? I think you're playing funny. I didn't see you do it.
J: What?
I: I didn't see you take any clay away and put it in the other one.
J: You just—you just—

(At this point, Janie combines both balls of clay and makes one big snake.)

I: Now it's bigger because you added some clay to it.
J: I took it from this ball. Did you see me?
I: Yes, I saw you.

In this interchange note the confidence Janie has in her perception of what is happening to the pieces of clay—that they actually changed in amount. We might say that she has a mental picture or image of reality: what looks bigger is bigger. In a very real sense, the structure of her mind has constructed reality, a world-view. She is so emotionally attached to it that she applies it even when it does not fit with her actions, apparently unaware of or unconcerned with the inconsistencies.

Nevertheless, enough doubt or conflict had been raised in Janie's mind so that two months later when we met again and repeated the same activity, she explained the change in amount in this way:

I: What did you do with the clay—the extra? If it doesn't have as much, what happened to it?
J: I smashed it.
I: Look how wide it is—it's much wider than the ball . . . fatter . . . see?
J: Mmmmmm. I'll make it into a ball.

36

I: Now what are they?

J: The same. I put it to its own self.

I: What does that mean?

J: I put it in the middle . . . Let's make snakes.

I: Okay . . . That's going to be a big fat snake. Does the snake have as much clay in it as the ball? Do they have the same amount of clay now?

(Janie shakes her head no.)

I: Which one has more?

(Janie points to the ball.)

I: Why?

J: 'Cause I'm making this into a snake.

I: Now they're two snakes. Do they have the same amount of clay in them?

J: Yes.

I: Why do you think that?

J: 'Cause they're all the same.

I: Smash one of them . . . Do they have the same amount of clay in them?

(Janie shakes her head no.)

J: I put this one to its own self.

Janie knew that she had not actually transferred any clay from one piece to another, but she was not ready to deny what she perceived as a change in the amount of clay. So she thought up the ingenious explanation that she had put the extra clay "to its own self, in the middle."

I have spent so much time with this description of Janie and the clay because it is basic to our understanding of how persons develop the structure of their thinking and reasoning, not only about physical objects, but about people, society, and moral issues. I would like to bring out the following points from the interview:

(1) Janie's mind held a picture or image of what she saw

as real and true, and she had a strong emotional attachment to this image.

(2) The combination of Janie's own interaction with the clay, plus talking about what happened and didn't happen, raised questions or conflict in her mind. This disturbed her certainty about the soundness of her perceptions; the balance of her perceptions was upset. It is such a process of interaction that upsets the equilibrium in the structure of thinking and may ultimately result in new structures. Janie's earlier concept of conservation of amount was then in disequilibrium and well on its way toward a new structure, as we shall see later.

During the *Preoperational Period* perceptions of the world still are not governed by logical laws and relationships. Perceptions are received quite naturally as a lot of disconnected pictures. From the child's viewpoint this is "the way life is." To be preoperational is to wonder at life and to trust that *anything* marvelous or bad can happen. While it is a time of fantasy, creativity, and imagination, inability to take the role of others and to make logical sense out of the world can be a serious liability and limitation in the areas of social perspective and moral reasoning.

The thinking of the preoperational child is summarized in the foldout chart.

SOCIAL PERSPECTIVE:
WAYS OF THINKING ABOUT PERSONS AND SOCIETY

The way a person constructs his or her understanding of the physical world—separation of the self from other objects and sensorimotor interaction with objects—is the basis for that individual's construction and interpretation of the world of persons and society. Consider the young boy who explains that the moon moves because it is following him. He may just as readily envision an omnipotent parent or deity watching him all the time and becoming angry when he tells lies, breaks something, or disobeys commands.

Or, consider Carlie who at 1½ years old painstakingly stuffed play dough into a small container. After several minutes of hard work, she proudly held up the full container and announced "Empty!" Her pleasure was obvious and pointed to the progress she was making in learning about her world. But it also points to the limitations of the simple structure that formed the basis for her organization of objects, actions, people, authority, rules, right and wrong. Her mind was just beginning to make connections among language, physical objects, and concrete action, but how much more complicated are the relationships in the world of people and society, the arena of social perspective.

Social perspective refers to the way in which a person relates to and perceives other persons and social structures —that is, how one conceives of the rules, laws, and governmental processes of a social system or structure. In my research, I have explored social perspective through the use of stories, moral dilemmas, and open-ended questions. The information obtained appears to organize itself into six subdivisions called "factors," and in examining a person's concepts of each factor, we receive insights into the development of social perspective. These six factors overlap and intertwine with one another in various ways at different stages, often prohibiting clear distinctions among them. Taken together, they do give at least a partial picture of how different world-views are constructed.

THE SIX FACTORS OF SOCIAL PERSPECTIVE
1. Concepts of persons—how they relate to one another and to society
2. Concepts of the value of human life
3. Role-taking ability—how well the person is able to put him or herself in the shoes of another person and interpret the thoughts and feelings of the other

4. Concepts of authority—where it lies, how it functions, how the person relates to it
5. Concepts of law—its function and purpose
6. Concepts of community and the structures of society and how persons relate to these

These factors of social perspective are indicated in figure 1. As with the development of logical thinking, persons appear to build increasingly complex ways of handling these six factors, based on interaction between their innate mental structures and the environment.

I use the same levels and stages that Kohlberg uses in his theory of moral reasoning to describe the development of social perspective. Each of the three levels consists of two stages. In the description of the young child we will be looking at what is called Stage 0, followed by Stage 1 in the **Preconventional Level**. In figure 1 see again how the levels and periods relate to each other. Note that Kohlberg's Stage 1 generally does not appear in children until near the end of Piaget's **Preoperational Period.**

Periods, levels, and stages are descriptive words, ways of organizing information. They are not labels to be put on individuals or boxes in which to stuff them. Neither do they constitute a scale of values by which to rate persons. But they do symbolize the increasingly complex worldviews that individuals construct on their developmental journeys.

In trying to describe each stage in light of the six factors of social perspective, I have discovered that different factors appear to predominate at different stages. Therefore, in the description that follows, I have varied the order of presentation of factors in order to build from the factor that appears to be most basic to a particular stage.

SOCIAL PERSPECTIVE—LEVELS/STAGES
STAGE 0

Concepts of Persons and of the Value of Human Life

Carlie(1½) and Janie(3) are playing with blocks at a low table. Carlie decides to wrap her arms around Janie in a big hug. Janie finds her own movements restricted and, annoyed, begins to squirm. Carlie hugs tighter. Janie yells in rage and flails about wildly. Carlie beams happily. She finds these results delightful and fascinating; for, as Piaget describes it, she loves to "keep interesting sights going."

At age 1½ the world is largely perceived as an undifferentiated conglomeration of objects and actions, as described in the *Sensorimotor Period*. People are seen as objects on which the child can act—and as objects which can react in particularly intriguing ways—giving the child pain or pleasure in return. With little ability to distinguish objects from living animals and people, it is no wonder that the small child is animistic and has no sense of the value of human and animal life in comparison with objects. At 1½, that which pleases most is of most value.

Role-Taking Ability

When Janie was 2½ I told her a story about a little girl who had promised her mother that she would not go out in the street. When the little girl's kitten runs out in the street, she has to decide whether to break her promise or to risk the injury or death of the kitten. I asked Janie:

"Should the little girl keep her promise to her mother or go out into the street to save her kitten?"

Janie's reply was:

"We put a leash on *our* dog 'cause we want to keep her so we can pet her."

In this answer we see four characteristics of the thinking of the young child.

First, there is no evidence of an understanding of the word "promise."

Second, although this child knows the difference between self and others, she has no comprehension that there are different points of view. Janie cannot relate to the situation of the little girl in the story from that child's viewpoint. She sees the whole story from her perspective

41

just as she did when I interviewed her about the doll taking pictures.

Third, Janie centers or fixates on one aspect that is important to her—the danger to the pet—which is characteristic of the *Sensorimotor and Preoperational Periods.*

Fourth, she displays typical egocentrism when she substitutes her own dog for the kitten. In addition, she shows no concern for the life or feelings of the pet, but rather for her own interests: "We want to keep her so we can pet her." The self is the center of the young child's world while all other people and animals are interesting objects. The child is unable to put him/herself in the place of another—to take the role of the other.

A familiar example is the occasion when the parent is not feeling well and asks the child to "Please be quiet so I can rest." Immediately there follows an unusual amount of noise or a series of unnecessary questions or unreasonable demands. This does not mean that the child is deliberately being inconsiderate. Rather, it signifies that the child's world has been upset and attention is needed. The child has no way of empathizing with— taking the role of—the parent.

Concepts of Authority, Law, and Community

The child learns from whatever authority, rules, and community structures are created by the persons in charge of him or her, but does not differentiate among them. However, the child's perceptions of authority as loving or cruel, reliable or capricious, are providing content for a developing world-view of authority, law, and community.

Summary of Stage 0

Related to Piaget's *Sensorimotor* and *Preoperational Periods*, Stage 0 describes a world-view in which the child stands at the center and is unable to perceive most of the logical relationships among people and society that we take for granted. At Stage 0, the child has only begun a lifelong journey of exploration. Through the structuring of perceptions in his or her mind, the child is making a path through the jungle. This clearing will shed light on further discoveries. Whatever else is perceived in the jungle will pass through the keyhole of the mind's structure at Stage 0. As adults, we may try to tell children how the world really is, but the child's world-view *is* the real world—the only real world for that child.

PRECONVENTIONAL LEVEL: STAGE 1

Stage 0 is sketchily defined because the language ability of small children is limited. However, during the *Preoperational Period* of logical reasoning children achieve some ordering of their physical world and gain facility in the use of language. This sets the stage for a more organized social perspective. The aspect of logical reasoning basic to Stage 1 is the ability to order concrete, physical things into series according to size because this allows the possibility of ordering social relationships according to physical qualities: age, size, strength, wealth, and power.

Concepts of Persons

I interviewed Bet 8, Janie 5, and Carlie, almost 4. I told them a story about two little girls who had broken some eggs. One of them had broken one egg while disobeying her mother; the other dropped a full carton while helping her mother make breakfast. I asked:

Which little girl was the worst? Do you suppose the mother was madder at one girl than the other?
Carlie: The mother was maddest at the littlest.
Interviewer: Do mommies get maddest at littlest girls?
C: Uh huh (yes).
I: Even though they're not as bad?
Janie: Yeah, they do all sorts of bad things.
I: What about bigger people?

Bet: Like me.

I: Yes, like you, Bet.

B: They do good things.

I: What about grownup people?

B: They do real good things.

J: They do goodest things.

These children hold a mental picture and perspective of the world in which people are divided into the physically bigger, older, stronger, and more powerful, in contrast with others who are smaller, younger, weaker, and powerless. It is not difficult to see how this concept of persons underlies the views of law, authority, community, and the value of human life expressed below.

Concepts of Law and Authority

One of the questions we asked in order to elicit information about social perspective was: *What is the law? What is its purpose or function?* Here are some typical answers from young children. "It's a thing you're not supposed to do. You get in trouble." "It's just a thing made up, if you don't do it you might get arrested or put in jail."

We then asked these children: *Would it be all right to break the law if you didn't get in trouble?*

Kathy at age 7 answered: No.

Interviewer: Why not?

K: Because it just wouldn't be right, it'd be bad, and God might see you and he can keep a track of everybody.

I: Oh, he can? What if he didn't see me do it? Could I do it then?

K: No, 'cause he can see everybody do everything.[6]

Janie at age 5 replied: It's all right to break the law if you're the boss, you won't get in trouble.

Interviewer: When you play that you are the boss, is it all right for you to break the law? You don't get in trouble?

J: I don't, 'cause I'm the boss.

I: Would it be all right for other people to break the law?

J: No way. They're not the boss.

From these conversations we get pictures of law and of authority which seem to revolve around the words "trouble" and "punishment." Law is seen as a prohibition which results in punishment if one is caught by an authority figure who, in the case of these children, is perceived as God or the boss. Parents, teachers, older siblings, babysitters, policemen (and other figures identified by uniforms) also fill this role of authority. Such an omnipotent figure is thought of as one who sees all and knows all, and whose demands and commands are not requests or options but factual, concrete realities—i.e., "The police has to put us in jail." There is apparently little distinction between law and authority; these concepts are not separated in Stage 1. The authority is a powerful person, and somehow the law is the same as this figure.

Concepts of Community and Society

We might make an informed guess at this point that a Stage 1 view of community and society would consist of a boss who decrees right and wrong and controls what goes on. An elementary school child presented such a picture when asked to write on the subject: *Why should my parents vote tomorrow?*[7] He wrote, "If there were no president there would be no freedom and there would be no representative and the world would be lost and there would be no names for any countrys or the state like Fort Worth."

As we read this sentence we may be impressed by the vocabulary and concepts, and then suddenly the whole view of the world collapses in chaos except for the power of the president! The confusion about geography adds an interesting insight into the child's picture: imagine what it might be like to drive into a completely strange city where there is no indication of street names, or traffic regulations. Perhaps this is what it is like to live in a Stage

1 world, with only the boss to keep order. (Confusion about geography will be discussed further in the next chapter.)

We can draw a simple picture to represent the structure of a Stage 1 social perspective in terms of law, authority, and concept of persons. At this stage, there is no concept of society as it is understood at later stages.

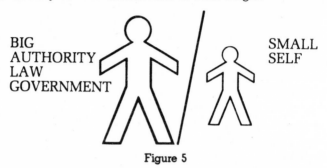

BIG
AUTHORITY
LAW
GOVERNMENT

SMALL
SELF

Figure 5

Role-Taking Ability

In the conversation about the broken eggs, note that the three children were not concerned with the intentions of the two little girls who broke the eggs. At Stage 1 attention is focused on concrete results and physical attributes rather than intentions or another's point of view. Children are largely egocentric and unable to understand differing points of view when they are not the same as their own or as that of persons in authority. However, children at Stage 1 begin to recognize that other people think and feel differently, and that people make decisions or do things for reasons of their own.

Concept of the Value of Human Life

One of the ways we explored concepts about the value of human life was through the use of two stories and sets of questions which invite comparison between the value of human and animal life. The stories and questions are given in Appendix A, Dilemma III, and in Appendix B. Here is one of the questions and two typical responses.

46

Q: *Which is more important or of more value, a sheep or a man?*

Kathy, 7: If a sheep is as old as a man it might be just as important.

Jody, 7: The man might be more important because a sheep is littler and the man's bigger.

The value of human life at Stage 1 is perceived in terms of age or size. When a Stage 1 perspective must deal with the choice of stealing or not stealing in order to save a human life, the decision is made on the basis of whether or not one "gets in trouble," "gets put in jail." There seems to be no value attached to human life itself.

Summary of Stage 1

In exploring Stage 1 in light of the six factors of social perspective, note the consistency of the child's world-view. All avenues or windows lead to the big-little dichotomy.

Some older children and adults retain this Stage 1 social perspective, even when their development in logical reasoning has progressed beyond the *Preoperational Period*. In such cases, the distinctions between power and powerlessness can become subtle and complex. They are no longer based on simple physical differences, but on personal perceptions and experiences of "who has control."

At Stage 1, the child's world-view has achieved some order and a basis for making distinctions of right and wrong, which was not possible at Stage 0. However, the limitations of Stage 1 include lack of role-taking ability, a simplistic division of all persons into big or little, and the use of that distinction as the basis for a concept of society and the value of human life.

MORAL REASONING:
WAYS OF THINKING ABOUT RIGHT AND WRONG

This section opens yet another window on the structure of the human mind, and again the window is composed of

divisions or issues whose concepts overlap and intertwine with one another as well as with the other divisions
we have explored (see figure 1). In this section I have
singled out a few of these issues in order to organize our
view of moral reasoning.

Moral *reasoning* is what the term implies: the *reasons*
one gives for what a person *should or ought* to do when
values are in conflict. It describes *how* an individual
determines what is right and wrong.

To review briefly, logical development refers to the
understanding of physical objects, to logical relationships among such objects, and to problem solving
involving such logic. It forms the underlying structure of
mental operations for the development of social perspective. And social perspective in turn provides the matrix
for the development of moral reasoning. In other words,
when confronted by a moral question, a person draws
upon his or her social perspective in reaching a decision
about what is right or wrong; although the subsequent
action or behavior may or may not be consistent with that
decision.

The role-taking factor in social perspective has been
explored through the research of Robert Selman. He has
found that people's stages in role-taking usually parallel
their stages in moral reasoning or exceed them by one
stage only. In no instance has he found that the stage in
moral reasoning exceeds the stage in role-taking. However, in a study of young-adult delinquents, for many of
the subjects development in role-taking exceeded development in moral reasoning by two or more stages.[8]

In this section, and in the following chapters for
succeeding age groups, I describe the stages in moral
reasoning as parallel to those in social perspective, thus
presenting a holistic picture of each segment of the
journey. The chart in figure 1 also reads this way.
However, in any one individual, either or both, the level
of social perspective and the level of moral reasoning can
straddle adjacent stages as a stable or a transitional

condition. I will include descriptions of such transitional experiences and structures. As we work with these models of the developmental journey, it is important to keep in mind that no one person "fits" into any model perfectly and that each human mind is an incredibly complex structure.

The same levels and stages are used to describe moral reasoning as those used for social perspective. However, the factors and issues are somewhat different.

STAGE 0

The world of the young child is not logical, and the child has no ability to take the role of others. There is no comprehension of the meaning of such words as "promise," "telling a lie," "stealing." At Stage 0 the child seems to have no concept of right or wrong other than "what I want." Small children do know that certain behavior may bring punishment and thus make some decisions about their behavior. Judy, at 11 months, pulls herself to a standing position at the coffee table piled with magazines. She puts one hand tentatively on a magazine and looks teasingly at her father. If he sternly says no, she bursts into tears. If he does not notice, she joyfully sweeps all the magazines onto the floor, and the repercussions are painful. Yet the resulting disapproval by her father carries no connotation of right and wrong. Any unpleasant result, such as getting bitten by a dog or burned by a hot stove, is simply a painful experience to be avoided. In the absence of physical repercussions, children make decisions according to what they feel like doing.

But the transition from Stage 0 to Stage 1 evolves from very concrete experiences of punishment and trouble related to "big" persons in the child's life. Punishment and trouble can be either emotional or physical, but it is interesting that children often associate punishment with the physical, even when they themselves have not been punished in a physical way.

An example of the kind of experience which stimulates

transition comes from an interview with Carlie at the age of 3 years, 10 months.

> Interviewer: What do you think about lying, Carlie? What do you think a lie is?
> Carlie: Ummmmm, it's not true.
> I: Do you ever tell lies? (C: shakes her head no.) Why not?
> C: Because.
> I: Because why?
> C: Just because.
> I: Is it naughty to tell a lie? (C: nods yes.) Why is it naughty to tell a lie?
> C: Ummmmm . . . because you get your mouth washed out.
> I: You get your mouth washed out?
> C: With soap.
> I: Did your mommy do that? (C: nods no.) She never did that to you? Who told you that?
> C: I just knowed because one day Ronnie told a lie, his mother wash-ted his mouth out with soap.

Here Carlie has developed some understanding of what a lie is. She relates it to one very concrete experience of trouble and punishment. She has not yet generalized from this one instance to a concept of "trouble and punishment by an authority" as making something wrong, but she has taken a big step into the next stage.

PRECONVENTIONAL LEVEL: STAGE 1

At Stage 1 of social perspective there is little ability to take the role of others, and one's world-view is oriented around the concept of authority. These factors are reflected in the decisions and judgments of Stage 1 moral reasoning.

Several children were asked the question: *Is it all right to tell a lie?* Here are some of the answers.

> Jody, age 7: No, it would get you into more trouble.
> Kathy, age 7: No, because people might get a little mad at you.

50

Interviewer: If nobody gets mad at you, would it be all right?

K: Maybe.

Janie, age 5: No, because you get in trouble.

Interviewer: And is it all right if you don't get in trouble?

J: It's all right. If you don't get in trouble, it's all right.

Kohlberg uses moral dilemmas in order to elicit moral reasoning. A moral dilemma is a story that involves a choice between conflicting values. Probably the best known of Kohlberg's moral dilemmas is the story of Heinz (see Appendix A, Dilemma III), which goes as follows:

In Europe, a woman was near death from a special kind of cancer. There was one drug that the doctors thought might save her. It was a form of radium that a druggist in the same town had recently discovered. The drug was expensive to make, but the druggist was charging ten times what the drug cost him to make. He paid $200 for the radium and charged $2000 for a small dose of the drug. The sick woman's husband, Heinz, went to everyone he knew to borrow the money, but he could only get together about $1000 which is half of what it cost. He told the druggist that his wife was dying, and asked him to sell it cheaper or let him pay later. But the druggist said, "No, I discovered the drug and I'm going to make money from it." So Heinz got desperate and broke into the man's store to steal the drug for his wife.

Persons reasoning at Stage 1 give reasons centering around punishment. The first question asked is: Should Heinz steal the drug? Why?

Some say that Heinz *should* steal the drug because: "You'll get in trouble if you let your wife die." or "People will be mad at you if you let your wife die."

Others say that Heinz *should not* steal the drug because: "You'll get put in jail." or "You'll get in more trouble."

Note that the actual decisions that people carry out DO NOT directly indicate the stage of reasoning; it is the *reasons* given about what is right and wrong that offer clues to the stage, or the *structure* of reasoning. At Stage 1, trouble is the reason given in support of both pro and con answers.

At Stage 1, the replies to questions about the Heinz dilemma show little ability to take the role of any of the characters in the story. No concern is expressed for anyone's feelings or rights. The decision is made on the basis of concrete consequences related to trouble or punishment. In Stage 1 moral reasoning, something is wrong if—you get caught, you are punished, somebody gets mad at you—if a lot of trouble or mess is the result. For instance, breaking a dozen eggs accidentally usually is worse than breaking one egg on purpose because more physical mess is the result. Little consideration is given to intentions.

According to Kohlberg, moral reasoning is an expression of one's concept of justice. The justice structure at Stage 1 is a relatively simple one: the small or weak should obey the strong, the strong should punish the small if they disobey. Authority as embodied in big or powerful individuals personifies right and wrong, morality, conscience. In a satirical article on the Watergate affair, a person who had been indicted for a crime was quoted as saying: "In retrospect, I guess it was stupid, not because we did it but because we were caught."[9] Conscience is experienced simply as the fear of punishment, so laws and rules are obeyed just in order to avoid punishment. At Stage 1, in the absence of authority, moral decisions are made on the basis of what the person feels like doing, as was true at Stage 0.

A WARNING

At this point the reader may be thinking: "I sometimes do things I know are wrong, like breaking the speed limit, if I think I won't get caught. Does this mean that I am using Stage 1 reasoning?"

The question to ask yourself is: *Why do I think it is wrong to speed?* Here are some possible answers:

—Because somebody might get hurt.

—It can be irresponsible to risk lives.

—It sets a poor example.

—We shouldn't take the law into our own hands. What if everybody were to do it? Laws keep order in society.

—I would get a ticket.

Only the last statement, if accompanied by little or no understanding of the other reasons, might be indicative of Stage 1 reasoning. The other statements, while not clearly related to particular stages, suggest more complex social perspectives than those found at Stage 1.

Decisions of a moral nature may be based on a variety of elements: emotional involvement, information, practical considerations, willpower, ego strength, and moral reasoning. All these are important and influence ultimate decisions and behavior. But in the sections of this book describing moral *reasoning*, I am dealing only with that specific part of the decision-making process that involves reasoning. How other concerns influence outcomes will be discussed in chapter 7.

SUMMARY

This chapter has described the ways in which young children think from three different dimensions: logical reasoning, social perspective, and moral reasoning. In the logical dimension, children may begin to move beyond preoperational thinking any time from age 4 or 5 through age 7 or 8. Stage 1 social perspective and moral reasoning may begin between ages 4 and 6. In some individuals it may continue to be used throughout adulthood.

In the next chapter we will be looking at the third period of logical reasoning—the Period of Concrete *Operations*—and at the social perspective and moral reasoning which it makes possible.

QUIZ

How are you doing? Take a look at the foldout at the back of the book and check yourself with these statements.

Column A	Column B
1. Thinking during the *Sensorimotor Period* develops through the child's activity of _____	1. big-little dichotomy
2. Egocentrism means that the child experiences _____	2. representation
3. A major advance of the *Preoperational Period* is in the ability to use _____	3. language
4. Ability to engage in the activity of deferred imitation is one of three characteristics of _____	4. logical reasoning development
5. Development of social perspective is based on _____	5. acting on objects
6. The basis of all structural development is _____	6. self as the center of the world
7. Stage 1 is characterized by the _____	7. moral reasoning
8. Social perspective provides the basis for the development of _____	8. interaction between innate mental structure and environment

ANSWERS

1. 5   2. 6   3. 3   4. 2   5. 4   6. 8   7. 1   8. 7

CHAPTER III
The Bookkeeper

INTRODUCTION

In this chapter we take a look at the period in the developmental journey when the "child of wonder" becomes a "young bookkeeper," filled with an urgency for making things come out even. This is the *Period of Concrete Operations*, which has been added to the chart below. Logical reasoning is explored through descriptions of its divisions, called "operations," which are performed differently within each period. These operations include:

seriation
conservation
classification
logical addition and multiplication
reversibility
decentration
perspective-taking

Viewpoints ("Windows")	Divisions	Periods . . . Levels/Stages		
Moral Reasoning	*Issues* Life Law etc.	Stage 0	Preconventional Level	
			Stage 1	Stage 2
Social Perspective	*Factors* Authority Law etc.	Stage 0	Preconventional Level	
			Stage 1	Stage 2
Logical Reasoning	*Operations* Conservation Seriation Reversibility etc.	Sensorimotor Period Age 0-1½	Preoperational Period Age 1½–7	Period of Concrete Operations Age 6 →

Figure 1

Concrete operations make possible new perceptions of the social world which in turn lead to new ways of making

55

moral decisions. These new developments in social perspective and moral reasoning will be described under the category of Stage 2.

LOGICAL REASONING:
THE PERIOD OF CONCRETE OPERATIONS

Eight months after her session with the clay described earlier Janie was interviewed again, at the age of 3 years, 10 months. Here is the record of that conversation.

Interviewer: See if you can make two balls of clay, just the same size. . . . There . . . are these the same size?
Janie: Yeah.
I: Do they have the same amount of clay in them?
J: Yeah.
I: Now, you pick one up, will you? Do you want to smash it or make a snake out of it?
(Janie smashes one of the balls.)
I: Does it have the same amount of clay in it as the ball, or a different amount?
J: Yeah, the same.
I: They don't look the same. Why do you think they have the same amount?
J: This one's smashed but this one's big, but it has the same amount.
I: Why does it have the same amount?
J: Because it's the same amount as this only though it's smashed.
(Janie makes a snake)
J: Anyway, it's into a snake and it has the same amount.
I: You're sure about that.
(Janie nods yes.)
I: Do you know that you didn't used to say that? Do you remember what you used to say?
J: No.
I: You used to say that the one that was smashed didn't have as much clay in it. Do you remember that?
J: When I was a little baby?

Janie's perception of reality appears to be changing to the extent that she cannot remember that it was different. However, she seems unable to explain clearly what is involved in her understanding of conservation of amount.

During the next interview, just after her fifth birthday, she answered this way.

J: They have the same amount.
I: Why do you think that?
J: Because they *were* the same size, and they still have the same amount.
I: But they look different. But you still think they have the same amount? Even 'though one is taller than the other?
J: *(Janie places the smashed ball on edge.)* When this is standing up it's taller. Ha, ha.

Janie's mental picture or image concerning conservation of amount indicates a permanent change in the structure of her thinking.

Thinking of the experience with the clay as if it were a stimulus from the environment, we can see that Janie was initially distorting what most adults perceive as reality. Her perception of the stimulus was shaped by the structure or "keyhole" in her mind. This is what Piaget calls "assimilation," the bending of reality to fit the shape of the structure.

When Janie encountered a conflict between what she perceived and what she actually was doing, her thinking process was triggered. The result was a change in her mental structure, a change necessary in accommodation to the new information she was receiving. This process is what Piaget calls "accommodation," the bending of the keyhole or structure to fit new perceptions of reality. According to Piaget these two processes, assimilation and accommodation, are the basis for development in logical reasoning. "The balancing of the processes of assimilation and accommodation may be called 'adaptation.' Such is the general form of psychological equilibrium."[1]

Developmental Journey

The process of adaptation creates increasingly complex structures, each of which is a closer adaptation to physical reality. Each new and more complex structure involves greater flexibility in accommodating or altering the structure in order to solve new problems as they appear.

As Janie began to perceive conservation of amount, she was starting that part of her journey characterized by the ability to think logically which Piaget calls the *Period of Concrete Operations*. However, she still had a long way to go before she was able to use concrete thinking for all of the operations. For instance, she continued to have difficulty arranging the seven straws in a series without careful trial and error and lining them up at the bottom.

Harry, first interviewed at age six, rapidly placed the seven straws in a series with no guesswork (figure 2). Performing this concrete operation is characteristic of the ability to think logically.

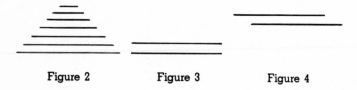

Figure 2   Figure 3   Figure 4

In another interview, two straws of equal length are placed side by side with the ends even (figure 3). The child, who is asked if the two straws are of the same length, in most cases will agree that they are, although sometimes only after checking carefully. One of the straws is then moved ahead of the other (figure 4), and the child is asked if the straws are still the same length. Harry 6 and Janie 5 were both very clear that the two straws did not change in length when simply moved out of alignment. However, two eight year olds, Bet and Kathy, said that the length changed. They had not yet achieved the operation called conservation of length. On the other

58

hand, Kathy's understanding of perspective (the little doll and the mountains) was more complex than that of Harry or Janie.

We need to recognize such variations in developing structures if we are to avoid categorizing persons and placing them in neat boxes. We are identifying thought patterns, not labeling persons. Each individual moves at his or her own pace in widely varying ways and may be well into a new structure in regard to some concepts while still comfortably entrenched in a simpler structure in others. We find this same situation when we examine social perspective and moral reasoning. The long journey is the same, but people move through it in many differing styles. It is as if we were following a path or road through a dense jungle, each of us clearing our own path and widening it as we go. Some may stop to savor the interesting things already discovered; others may concentrate on clearing the path ahead. Eventually many stop exploring and live within the clearing they have already constructed.

Piaget suggests that taking time is important. In my classes I have recently been using a poster depicting massive rocks rising from a turbulent river with the caption "Things Take Time." This expresses my conviction that learning, whether it be a change in structure or internalization of information (adding Xs to present structure), requires patience and time. The emphasis of our culture on "bigger and better and farther and faster" may not be the most effective way to stimulate in-depth learning and development. If we will see time as our ally in the developmental journey, it will give us the vision to accept where we and others are in our journeys.

For instance, although Janie could understand conservation of amount by age 5, most children in our culture achieve this by ages 7 or 8. Such variation is normal and may depend more on particular stimulating experiences than on differences in intelligence. It will take perhaps two more years of experiences for a child to understand conservation of weight and two years beyond that for conservation of volume. Applying one operation, such as conservation, to solve additional tasks at one level is what Piaget calls "horizontal décalage."[2] The child also needs to learn other operations within the context of concrete operations, such as seriation and classification. There is considerable evidence to indicate that concentration on décalage and broadening within a stage or period may be of more value to the individual's ultimate development than is untimely pressure to move to the next level. "Things take time."

The primary intellectual task of children during the *Period of Concrete Operations* is to learn the logical relationships among the objects and actions which they first "acted upon" *(Sensorimotor Period)* and then "represented" *(Preoperational Period)*. During the *Period of Concrete Operations,* children discover how to organize and classify those objects and actions which can be seen, heard, tasted, felt, or otherwise experienced in *concrete* ways. Thus we talk about concrete operations. This is a time when what cannot be seen and proven is to be neither trusted nor believed.

At this period, usually found in children after the age of seven, the child cannot form hypotheses nor imagine possibilities other than those perceived in concrete and direct ways. One woman related an incident about her eight-year-old son who usually came home from school for lunch. One day he was instructed to eat at school because his mother was going out. The boy forgot, arrived home and found the house locked. He broke a window with a rake handle, went inside and made a sandwich, then went back to school. Later in the day his horrified mother questioned him about why he had done such a thing, but it was obvious that he did not understand why she was so upset. He said that he had come home for lunch, and since the food was inside the house, he had needed to get in in order to eat. It had never occurred to him that there might be alternative ways of solving the dilemma. He had taken what for him was the only logical, sensible action. He was unable to generate other possibilities. His mother was relieved to learn that this was a normal way of thinking for an eight-year-old, but she realized that she had better outline some other options for the boy in case such a situation arose again!

At this point I will describe several other concrete operations without attempting to include all the characteristics or all the operations. More complete information can be found in books listed at the end of the book.[3]

One operation, perspective-taking, which is particularly significant for development of social perspective, can be demonstrated using the task of the little doll and the mountains. The child who becomes aware that the doll, when placed in different positions, actually sees a different view than he or she does, is beginning to use concrete operations. At first, the child chooses only some

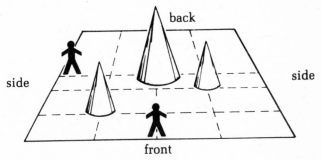

Figure 5

of the correct pictures because his or her structure is not sufficiently developed to permit adequate coordination of front-back and side-to-side perspectives for all positions (figure 5). But at the highest level of concrete operations the child can perform this task repeatedly and accurately. In tests reported by Laurendeau and Pinard, one quarter of the twelve-year-old subjects were able to resolve perfectly all the problems in the test.[4] The development of such logical perspective-taking ability with the concrete task of seeing what another person sees prepares the child intellectually to anticipate what another might be thinking or feeling.

Concepts of time also develop gradually. Anyone who has taken a long trip with a child has probably engaged in the following kind of conversation.

Child: When are we going to get there?

Adult: Not for a long time. It takes about six hours. We'll be there in time for supper.

(Five minutes pass)

Child: Are we there yet?

During this period, only concrete experiences of time make sense to children because they are just learning to organize what is immediately present. It will take time to solidify concepts of "tomorrow" and "yesterday" so that they make sense. A clear idea of historic time cannot be grasped until the child has developed a structure of thinking more complex than that involved in concrete operations. Understanding geographical distinctions also begins to develop during this period. At age six, Janie said that "Denver and Colorado and the United States are all the same size." Eight-year-old Kathy said that "I can't live in both Denver and Colorado at the same time" and that "Europe is maybe a country." Both these girls have worked with maps and have heard the distinctions discussed, but neither yet has the ability to form the mental images which organize these rather abstract ideas. This ability will develop toward the end of the period. An inference for educators, both in secular and religious settings, is that they keep in mind the slow development of concepts of time and geography. Otherwise, instruction involving these concepts may result in confusion and inaccuracy, surely not the goal of teachers.

Although I have suggested a normal age range for the *Period of Concrete Operations* in educationally and technologically advanced societies, there is considerable variation among normal children, as we have seen in the examples cited. Despite the typical range, it is possible to find learning difficulties in adolescents which can be attributed to inadequate achievement of concrete operations. This deficiency may not be due to any innate slowness in the individals, but rather to a lack of appropriate stimulation from the learning environment. Another consideration inherent in the educational procedures and aims appropriate to technologically oriented societies is that while they stimulate the use of concrete operations, they may also limit development of logical reasoning to that level. Concrete operational thinking is the highest level of development attained by many adults in the United States, as will be described later.

Piaget has described the person who thinks in terms of concrete operations as a "sober book-keeperish organizer of the real, distruster of the subtle, the elusive, the hypothetical."[5] It is a time of logically ordering physical reality, of "sticking to concrete facts," of needing to "see it in order to believe it." During this period there is a great advance over preoperational thinking, in terms of the preparation of structures for new developments in social perspective and moral reasoning. The person who thinks concretely has constructed a larger and more orderly clearing in the jungle, but the light is still limited. There is an inability to hypothesize about what might be. At this level of social perspective one cannot stand back and look at one's self "thinking about thinking" and reflect on this. The concrete operational world is confined largely to physical reality as it is seen, felt, heard, and otherwise proven to exist.

The *Period of Concrete Operations* is summarized in the foldout chart.

SOCIAL PERSPECTIVE

The "sober book-keeperish organizer of the real" is moving into a world where things are in order, where there are logical sequences of cause and effect, where "the books must balance," and everything must be fair. This makes possible a new and different social perspective, which we see emerging in the following six factors, described at Stage 2.

PRECONVENTIONAL LEVEL: STAGE 2

Concepts of Law

To review, the question asked in all our interviews probing social perspective was: *What is the law? What is its purpose or function?*

Here are some answers classified as Stage 2: "It's so people don't go breaking into places and going around just shooting everybody in the middle of the street." "If everybody broke the law you wouldn't have any right people around—there'd be all killings." "Laws are so people don't kill and do anything bad."

Janie, at age six years and three months, answered the question thus: "Laws are so people don't steal and have car crashes." This is quite different from her statement made at age five: "It's a thing you're not supposed to do. You get in trouble."

If we compare these answers with those given at Stage 1, we find that they have little in common. Missing here are the references to punishment or trouble inherent in the law at Stage 1. Rather, we see a picture of killing, stealing, and car crashes, concrete destructive acts which are prevented by law. In our research, the children who gave these second responses ranged in age from six to thirteen years. They were well aware of the consequences of breaking the law in terms of punishment and jail sentences, but saw such results as inconveniences to be avoided rather than as inherent in the law itself.

Value of Human Life

The statements about law do not construct a simple picture of social perspective as did the Stage 1 responses. Concepts of the value of human life give additional clues. I have tried to build the total perspective for each stage in a logical manner through the order of presentation of the six factors, and since each stage tends to emphasize different factors, the order I use varies.

> Question: (see Appendix B) *Which is more important or of more value, a man or a sheep?*
> Answers: "A man is more important than a sheep because a man can do more things."
> "I think a sheep could probably do some things that a person can, yeah, I think a sheep's as important as a man."
> "A person is more important than an animal. You can do more stuff than an animal—work—animals don't work as much as humans."

People and animals are prized according to the number of things they can do, the more valuable being the ones with the most abilities. It is as if a ledger sheet were being kept, and the value of a person or animal depended on the number of entries accumulated for useful activities or abilities performed. Here we see the pervasive significance of the book-keeper approach to social perspective.

Role-Taking Ability

Eleven-year-old Kathy, when asked about the relative value of human and animal life, answered: "I like a lamb better because a man probably wouldn't get to play with you, probably do all this work. . . . He'd be important, but he probably wouldn't have any time to do anything . . . the lamb is playful."

Kathy's remarks demonstrate a continuing egocentrism: the value of the man or the animal is in terms of the child herself and what they can do for her. We find another example of this in chapter 1 as part of a discussion of the Heinz dilemma. A student gave this response to a question about the rightness of stealing to save Heinz's wife: "I think it depends on how much the man needs his wife. If he doesn't like her, why risk getting thrown in jail? Let her die, and then get a new wife." In this case, the value of the wife is in terms of her usefulness to her husband and *her* viewpoint is not considered.

When asked about the value of life and what she meant by a good life, Kathy answered: "A life of a person is very important. . . . Like if someone had a nice life and played with some of his friends, played football or whatever he or she liked to do, you know, running around and everything . . ." Here Kathy appears to demonstrate a recognition that different persons might have different points of view about what makes up "a good life," although she still orients herself from a child's perspective. Her new awareness relates to the intellectual understanding of the differing perspectives of the little doll and the mountains. At Stage 2, a person has developed the reasoning ability to know that persons think differently from the self, to apprehend the intentions of others, and to recognize that others have their own views of themselves as individuals.

Concepts of Persons

What emerges from these quotations is a picture of persons valuing others in terms of usefulness to themselves primarily, with some recognition that usefulness to others is also important. The Stage 2 perspective is still primarily egocentric and ascribes to others the same self-interest and egocentricity that controls one's own social perspective. Persons are perceived as equal individuals, each with a distinguishable point of view, with an inherent right to "do one's own thing" and to meet one's own needs. This strongly influences moral reasoning, as we shall see in the next section.

Concepts of Authority

Since all persons are perceived as "out for themselves," those in authority are often seen as egocentric individuals bent on serving their own interests. "They're just doing it (*enforcing the law*) because they want to be the big cheese." "You're only making me do that because *you* don't want to be bothered."

Authority is acknowledged, however, in individuals who are known personally, who have earned respect through ability, and whose values are not too different from those of the self. During Stage 2, egocentrism and the tendency to reject authority create unique problems, especially for adolescents.

Concepts of Community and Society

A Stage 1 answer to the question *Why should my parents vote tomorrow?* was quoted in Chapter 2. Another elementary school child evidenced additional development in this response.[6] "What if someone got lazy and didn't vote and someone is elected you don't like; it's your fault. So vote and they might choose the one you like." In this answer there is an awareness of personal responsibility although it is directed, not toward the good of society, but toward achieving one's own ends. But a completely new structure, providing a basis for relationships between equal individuals, is demonstrated by Janie's explanation at age six of why stealing is wrong: "How would you like it if you worked hard and got a bunch of stuff and somebody stole it? That isn't fair."

This is a statement of the Stage 2 perspective that fairness and honesty in relationships are essential in order to protect each individual's interest. It is expected that others will not be deceitful about specific, concrete information and personal possessions. Lying and breaking promises are not fair because they destroy implicit bargains. But if the other person does it first, it may be fair to reciprocate in kind. As Janie said, "My friend's mother told us if those other kids told secrets we could do it back at them." "Do unto others as they do unto you." is the Golden Rule at Stage 2. Altruism toward others is based largely on the expectation of return of favors or services. All exchanges must be kept equal and require a running balance of services or goods given and received. The "book-keeper" has plenty of work at Stage 2!

This way of relating to other persons is the first mutual

relationship possible for the developing child, and it is called *dyadic* (two-way) *instrumental* (useful). Such a relationship operates in the economic system where there is an exchange of money for goods and where honest transactions are necessary in order to keep people from being cheated.

The image of the economic system is useful in depicting a Stage 2 concept of community or society: isolated equal individuals centered on self-interest, with fairness and law functioning to protect that self-interest and to prevent concrete destructive behavior (killing and stealing and car crashes). For the first time, there is a structure which regulates relationships between two people of equal status and which controls one-to-one relationships (figure 6).

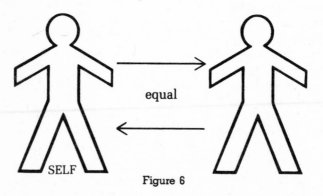

Figure 6

At Stage 2, the world-view, the clearing in the jungle, has expanded from Stage 1 to include new ways of relating to other persons, and new perceptions of how and what one values. But again it has its limitations. Role-taking ability is limited, and there is as yet no concept of an overarching societal structure. Human life has only a very utilitarian value, and egocentrism still functions strongly.

Stage 2 may begin as early as age six and is common during the junior high years. It is the way the world is structured for some adults. For many people a Stage 2 view is the real world.

MORAL REASONING

PRECONVENTIONAL LEVEL: STAGE 2

When Janie was 4 years old, she responded to the dilemma of breaking a promise vs. saving the kitten's life by explaining: "You shouldn't break the promise 'cause you'll get in trouble." But when she was almost six, she said: "You should save the kitten's life, that's more important, 'cause getting a spanking isn't that bad." In this transitional example and the one described earlier of Carlie and lying, it is possible to discern how the very concrete experiences of the young child influence the development of their social perspective and moral reasoning. In the second response, Janie is using an actual physical experience as a basis for questioning her Stage 1 moral reasoning. The door is opening for the development of her reasoning, but at that interview she was not yet able to give any Stage 2 reasons. Later however, at age 6 years, 3 months she was consistently giving Stage 2 reasons. If we refer back to the high school student quoted at the beginning of chapter 1, we can see that the student gave a Stage 2 answer to the question *Should Heinz steal the drug? Why?*: "I think it depends on how much the man needs his wife. If he doesn't like her, why risk getting thrown into jail? Let her die and then get another wife." In this answer, the student's justification for or against stealing depended on the usefulness or instrumentality of the wife to the husband, characteristic of Stage 2. A twelve-year-old boy answered in this way: "Stealing is unfair to the other person, and, like say, he broke into the man's store and took all his money, then he could die without any money. So it'd keep going, and he might steal from someone else." Here is a typical Stage 2 perspective of law, concern for concrete destructive acts and their results, and the limitation at the concrete operational period in being able to generate alternative solutions to the problem. (If the druggist's money is taken, he has no alternative but to go out and steal.)

This same boy says that the druggist had the right to charge so much for the drug because: "He invented it, it's his right to either raise the price or lower it, but it would be wise to lower it because he might be able to get in trouble, you know, like be robbed. It's not really right for him to charge that much unless he's desperate, too, and he needs the $2000 awfully fast." This boy demonstrates the ability to see different points of view in a concrete way which was not evident at Stage 1. He refers to "getting in trouble," not as a moral reason, but as a practical kind of inconvenience resulting from raising the price.

The justice structure at Stage 2 is defined as equal exchange between two individuals, exemplified in such unique interpretations of the Golden Rule as, "Do unto others as they do unto you," and "You scratch my back, I'll scratch yours." Each person is responsible for his/her own possessions and needs and has no obligation to others except when fairness of exchange (primarily to benefit the individual's own needs) enters the picture. This outlook is expressed in the statement, "Do your own thing." These are all manifestations of explicit egocentricity and the limited role-taking ability of Stage 2. Conscience may be experienced as "being chicken," "being afraid of the police," and the sense of guilt is mild and tends to be ignored. "It's not my problem, I'm not going to get involved," is a *moral* justification in Stage 2 thinking.

In response to the Heinz dilemma, here are some pro and con answers with characteristic moral reasoning at Stage 2:

Pro: Heinz should steal the drug:

—if he needs his wife
—if he needs the drug more than the druggist needs the money

—because the druggist was cheating him, wasn't being fair, and deserved to be stolen from

Con: Heinz should not steal the drug:

—if he doesn't want to keep his wife
—if he doesn't want to go to jail and give up his freedom or be inconvenienced; if it's not worth the risk
—because it's not fair to the druggist who should be able to charge what he wants because he made the drug

These examples demonstrate how Stage 2 moral reasoning can be used to support either a pro or a con position and why one cannot use the conclusion of a particular decision to determine the stage.

Stage 2 reasoning might, for instance, be used to justify support of the Equal Rights Amendment on the basis of "women should be able to do what they want." It might oppose the ERA because "women are useful to men," OR because "women should be protected from doing certain things which are troublesome or inconvenient to them." A letter to a newspaper stating the writer's reason for opposing the ERA gave some evidence of this last perspective: "I am glad I don't have to do a man's manual labor or factory job and work the long hours of compulsory overtime that they do."[7] This statement can be a simple expression of feeling, but when used as it was here to support a stand on a moral issue, it takes on the connotation of moral reasoning.

Stage 2 reasoning is found occasionally in children as young as six or seven years of age and is very common in elementary grades and junior high school. It is not uncommon in adult reasoning.

SUMMARY OF THE PRECONVENTIONAL LEVEL

Stages 1 and 2 are grouped together in what Kohlberg calls the **Preconventional Level** used to designate both social perspective and moral reasoning. At this level, the individual is beginning the process of interaction with moral and social realities of the environment, but there

71

appears to be little understanding or acceptance of the normal social processes or conventions. The center of the preconventional world-view is the SELF, a concrete individual perspective. Basic characteristics of this level are egocentrism and inability to take the roles of other persons except in the most concrete and pragmatic ways. These features impose severe limitations on how an individual can understand and resolve moral issues.

Kohlberg and Scharf have described the moral thinking of participants in the Mylai incident of the Vietnam War, demonstrating how moral reasoning can effect the decisions of men placed in a position calling for violent actions.[8] Paul Meadlow, a soldier who had admitted his involvement in killing civilians at Mylai, was interviewed on CBS television on November 24, 1969. Kohlberg and Scharf "very tentatively attempt to 'stage' the moral logic used" by Meadlow to explain why, on orders from Lieutenant Calley, he fired upon the civilians. They describe his thinking, revealed in the interview and in the testimony given at the Calley trial, as appearing

to be primarily at the preconventional level of moral thought: Stage 1 or 2. For example, his conception of authority appears to be a Stage 1 notion of blind obedience to power. . . . Meadlow's conception of retribution is equally primitive. He believes that it was right to "waste" the Vietnamese in order to get "satisfaction" and in terms of an equally primitive Stage 1 notion of revenge:

"Why did I do it. . . .We was supposed to get satisfaction from this village for the men we lost. They was all VC and VC sympathizers.

I felt, at the time, I was doing the right thing because, like I said, I lost buddies. I lost a damn good buddy. . . ."[9]

Meadlow seemingly has little intuition that what he has done offends even conventional moral sensibilities. He has only the barest understanding that killing babies is not normally seen as acceptable conduct:[10]

Q: You married?

A: Right. Two children. The boy is two and one-half, the girl is one and one-half.

Q: Obviously the question comes to my mind . . . the father of two little kids like that. How can he shoot babies?

72

A: I didn't have the little girl. I just had the little boy at the time.

Q: Uh huh. How do you shoot babies?

A: It's just one of those things.[11]

In chapter 5, I will use the response of another Mylai participant as it relates to a different stage. Such examples suggest the relevance of reasoning to behavior.

Presentation of developmental theory usually raises many questions for students. Therefore, in chapter 4 we will pause to consider questions which may have been raised for the reader by these first chapters.

QUIZ

The quiz for this chapter takes a different form. Its purpose is to give you practice in using the information presented in chapters 2 and 3. These exercises were developed for use by students in classes on developmental theory and are generally worked on by small groups of participants. For the first one, read the dilemma and then try to answer the questions.

EXERCISE I

DEBBIE'S DILEMMA[12]

For her seventh birthday Debbie's father has promised to take her to the carnival. She may choose five rides as part of her present. Debbie and her father arrive at the park and walk along outside the fence to the ticket gate. They see many of the rides, hear the music, and even get to see part of a parade through the fence.

When Debbie and her father approach the gate to buy the tickets, Debbie's father discovers he has left his wallet at home. He has just enough change in his pocket for two admission tickets, but that means no money left over for rides. Debbie is very disappointed. She remembers that her friend Kathy told the ticket-taker she was still six years old long after she was really seven, and she got in for half price and got to go on more rides. Debbie tells her father that she could do the same, and there would be more money for rides. Debbie's father reminds her that if she did this, she would be telling a lie about her age.

Should Debbie lie or tell the truth? (Keep in mind that the issue is telling the truth or lying and is not how to get into the carnival.)

According to the theory, the question (*Should Debbie lie?*) can be answered either yes or no at each stage.

1. If Debbie reasons at Stage 1 what reasons might she give for:
   a. telling the lie?
   b. telling the truth?

2. If Debbie reasons at Stage 2 what reasons might she give for:
   a. telling the lie?
   b. telling the truth?

ANSWERS

At Stage 1, the structure of moral reasoning will be based on obedience to authority and staying out of trouble. Therefore, we might project the following kinds of reasons:

Pro (lie)
—it's okay if no one finds out (specifically, the ticket-taker)
—my daddy will be mad if we don't get to go
Con (not lie)
—the ticket-taker will be angry if he/she finds out
—my daddy will be mad if I tell a lie

What does this imply about the role of the parent of the child who is reasoning at Stage 1? It suggests that the way the parent chooses to behave—frustrated about not getting in, angry at the child's suggestion of lying, or calm in offering other possibilities—is critical in stimulating the child's moral reasoning.

At Stage 2, reasons will center on: fairness, importance to the wants or needs of an individual, avoidance of bad habits:

Pro (lie)
—Debbie and her daddy went to a lot of effort to go to the fair, and their fun will be spoiled if they don't get to go
—Kathy got in for less money, and it is only fair that Debbie gets to, also
Con (not lie)
—it's not fair if some people get in for less money while others pay full price
—it is important not to lie, because once you tell a lie it

might be easier to tell another one, and you might get the habit

EXERCISE II

This exercise is for those persons who are interested in the way social perspective relates to how one understands biblical material. However, this exercise also applies to other types of literature and to social documents such as the Constitution of the United States.

Task: Imagine that you are teaching a church school class of first and second graders who hold social perspectives of Stage 1 and Stage 2. You have just read them the story of Matthew 12:9-14 (see Appendix B), concluding with the statement: "And surely a man is of much more value than a sheep." You follow this reading with the question: *Which do you think is of more value, a man or a sheep?"*

At Stage 1, some children will think the man is more valuable, some will think the sheep. What kinds of reasons can you expect from these children to support each view?

a. The sheep is more important or of more value

b. The man is more important or of more value

At Stage 2, some children will think the man is more important, some will think the sheep. Again, what kinds of reasons might you expect to support each view?

a. In favor of the sheep

b. In favor of the man

ANSWERS

At Stage 1, children may respond from the standpoint of which is the older or bigger.

At Stage 2, children may respond from the standpoint of which is the most useful, has the most abilities, or on the replacement possibilities—"You can buy a new sheep, but not a new person." One junior high student gave a delightful reply: "The man (is of more value), 'cause the sheep can turn into lamb chops . . . in them days the only thing they used the sheep for was to eat and sprinkle the blood over the fence posts around the door. Well, let's see, I think they could probably do some things that a person can. I think the sheep's as important as a man, yeah."[13]

CHAPTER IV
A Pause for an Overview

We have explored the first steps in three strands of the human developmental journey which are classified under the overarching label—"cognitive development." Cognitive means to become acquainted with, to know. Technically, it refers to intellectual activities of the mind which include thinking, recognizing, remembering, perceiving, knowing, and generalizing. Sometimes the word "structural" is added to the term, and we have "cognitive structural development." Logical reasoning, social perspective, and moral reasoning are different segments of cognitive structural development. The fourth strand or segment, faith development, will be discussed using James Fowler's theory. The brevity of its presentation is not a measure of its importance, but a reflection of the paucity of published material available at the time of this writing.

We need to keep before us the idea that a person is a highly complex organism—that a person's cognitive, emotional, behavioral, physical, and other components involve intricate structures and processes which interact independently and in conjunction with one another. We can arrive at new understandings of persons by isolating and examining separate aspects, by looking at the whole room from the viewpoint of one window. But we must be careful to link cognitive development with the other vital cords.

In recent years the research of Robert Ornstein and others strongly suggests that the human mind operates through two distinct modes, possibly related to the two hemispheres of the brain.[1] One mode of functioning, commonly associated with the left hemisphere, is logical, verbal, rational, and analytical. The second mode, usually related to the right hemisphere, is metaphorical, spatial, imaginative, intuitive, and synthesizing. How these operations in the brain relate to developmental theory is not entirely clear, especially the right brain functioning. It has been suggested that imagination appears to play an integral part in the development of role-taking ability. Elizabeth Leonie Simpson suggests that higher levels of moral reasoning require imaginative thinking, that imagination allows the person to try out new points of view before actually acquiring them.[2] Correlations here await further research. Relationships between moral reasoning and behavior will be discussed later.

Kohlberg's research provides evidence that children's reasoning progresses in a way that can be described as a series of stages. The normal, growing organism tends to become increasingly complex and differentiated while at the same time achieving more integration. This progression appears to hold true for cognitive as well as physical growth, and it is not normally reversible. A cognitive stage is a consistent pattern of thinking, a structured whole, an organized system of thought in the developmental process of knowing. It is a way of describing a particular structure. One of my students says that it helps to think of structures and stages as neutral, as descriptions without value connotations.[3]

The stages are hierarchical, that is, each stage builds on the previous ones, incorporates them, and carries them forward in modified forms. Stages are also invariant, meaning that they cannot be skipped or reversed. And the same sequence of development has been seen in all cultures so far examined, which suggests that the stages are universal.

Although rates of change may vary drastically, there are no sudden jumps from a very simple to a very complex stage. The physical body cannot have a simple infantile structure one year and a complex mature form the next, with leaps back and forth between the two in subsequent years. Neither does cognitive growth take place in such an erratic fashion.

Some people, however, move faster and farther through the sequence of stages than do others. Development is the result of interaction between innate mental structure and stimulation from the environment, and environments vary. Kohlberg's research suggests that there are no differences in sequence of development of moral reasoning among Catholics, Protestants, Jews, Buddhists, Moslems, and atheists. Although the sequence is universal, the rate of change and the highest stages attained are not. The reasons for this are not entirely clear, but some environments seem to fix or put a ceiling on development at less complex levels than do others.

Cognitive development is a long-term process, and it is not automatic. Remember that Piaget stresses the importance of horizontal décalage, the broadening within a level, the mastery of many tasks within a particular stage. The person who learns to reason at Stage 1 about the issue of authority must still struggle with other issues such as life, punishment, truth, and law before a full Stage 1 structure is achieved. Piaget suggests that "cognitive change should be, roughly speaking, slow rather than fast."[4] Restructuring takes time!

Individuals appear to do most of their reasoning at one stage, or more commonly, at two adjacent stages. People seem to prefer the highest moral stage they can understand and usually cannot comprehend reasoning more than one stage above their own.[5]

Restructuring ways of knowing is stimulated by experiences of cognitive conflict, the exchange of varying views, exposure to the next stage of reasoning, and similar conflict-producing situations. I use the term "conflict" here to mean the inconsistencies and contradictions which are created in one's own thinking—such as Janie encountered in working with and attempting to explain the amount of clay in the two balls. In class discussions such as the one quoted in the introduction to this book, the students heard a variety of reasons from different stages. Students reasoning at Stage 3 often reject lower stage reasons as being less adequate than their own. But those same students will be attracted to Stage 4 reasons and feel challenged and confronted by them. It is such contradictions, or internal conflicts, that provide the links or steps leading to successively more complex structures.

The terms "structure" and "content" are used throughout the book, but the distinctions between them are not easily made. It takes practice, concentration, and correction to discern the structure of a person's reasoning as opposed to the content of the answer. An image I find helpful is the metaphor I have already used several times, the keyhole. As the child watches, listens to, and interacts with the world, experiences and perceptions enter the mind through a distinctive keyhole and are shaped by it. Envision the mind of a child with a Stage 1 social perspective; it is a world of big vs. little persons. Imagine that the keyhole has just such a distinctive shape as in figure 1. All stimuli from the environment will pass

Figure 1

through this distinctive keyhole or structure whose shape is identified by stages. At Stage 1, for instance, "law" is perceived in terms of big authorities who punish little people. A person at this stage may say "It is wrong to break the laws," but this tells us nothing about structure. We need to ask, "Why is it wrong to break the law?" and the answer may then reveal structure: "Because you get in trouble (with an authority figure)." The concept of law is understood at all stages, but in different ways. At higher stages the answers are different, and this is because stimuli have been shaped by a modified keyhole or structure.

Perhaps the easiest way to demonstrate differences between content and structure is to give some examples.

"Heinz should steal the drug."	*Content.* This is a decision or conclusion and reveals nothing about structure. It can be made at any stage.
"Stealing is against the law."	*Content.* This statement reveals nothing about structure and can be made at any stage.
"Breaking the law is wrong because you get put in jail."	*Structure.* This reveals something about how law is perceived through a distinct keyhole and has been shaped by it.
"I get very upset when someone breaks the law."	*Content.* Expresses feelings, emotions.
"I would never break the law."	Content. Decision, action, what one *would do*.
"Heinz is so selfish, he must be Stage 2."	This does not answer the question. It describes behavior or motives, but says nothing about moral reasoning. It is also a misuse of developmental theory, in that it labels the whole person rather than the reasoning.

Should and why questions are most apt to elicit moral reasoning structures: "What *should* Heinz do?" and "*Why* should he do it?" (What Heinz *would* do might not be what he *should* do.)

Probably the most effective way to achieve a functional understanding of the distinction between structure and content is through the discipline of scoring and scoring conferences. Interviewing and scoring form the basis for the description of developmental stages and for the understanding of their complexities; I will therefore give a brief introduction to the procedure. This description does not provide the necessary detailed instructions and materials to enable a person to actually interview and score, but it should give the reader an idea of how developmental stages are identified.

Scoring starts with the moral judgment dilemma and the interview which dwells on the kinds of questions that elicit reasons for the person's decisions and beliefs. See the Heinz dilemma and interview questions in Appendix A for an example of this.

In scoring, Kohlberg uses two different series of moral dilemmas, each consisting of three dilemmas, which are designed to elicit moral reasoning on different issues. For instance, the Heinz dilemma is used to probe for reasoning about the moral issues of life and law, the two major values or concerns which come into conflict in this dilemma. However, for some persons other issues may assume importance. For some, the moral conflict in this case is between life and property; for others, it is between law and affection.

Kohlberg lists eleven moral issues which he calls "values objects," (see the "divisions" of moral reasoning introduced in figure 1, chapter 2). He says that "a moral choice involves choosing between two or more of these values as they *conflict* in concrete situations of choice. . . . The stage or structure of a person's moral judgement defines 1) what he finds valuable in each of these moral issues (life, law), i.e., how he defines that value, and 2) why he finds it valuable, i.e., the reasons he gives for valuing it."[6] Here are Kohlberg's eleven moral issues.

1. Punishment	4. Authority
2. Property	5. Character
3. Affiliation (roles and concerns of affection)	6. Law
	7. Contract

8. Truth   10. Life
9. Liberties   11. (Sex)

A series of moral dilemmas and the interview questions are given in Appendix A. The questions are designed to elicit the individual's reasoning about the issues. The interviews are tape recorded because it is very important to have the person's exact wording when transcribing them. Here is an example of an interview, one of my favorites, done with Janie when she was 6 years, 4 months.

1. *Do you think that Heinz should steal the drug?*
   No.
2. *Why Not?*
   Because it's bad to steal.
3. *Why is it bad to steal?*
   You might get in jail, and it doesn't belong to you so you shouldn't take it.
4. *Why shouldn't you take it if it doesn't belong to you?*
   'Cause it's somebody else's and it might cost lots of money and they made it theirselfs and stuff. So you shouldn't steal it.
5. *Which do you think is worse, letting someone die . . . letting that lady die . . . or stealing the drug? Which is the worst?*
   I don't think he should steal. Maybe he could go around the whole town and get some money.
6. *He tried to do that, and he couldn't get it. He had to have it right away or his wife might die.*
   Why didn't he go over and over again?
7. *Well, he tried that and he couldn't get it.*
   Over and over?
8. *Yes, he tried over and over. That's what it said. He tried everything he knew, but he couldn't get it. Do you still think that he shouldn't steal the drug? Even if his wife would die?*
9. *This is what the story says. If he can't get the drug*

his wife is going to die. So what do you think?
Well, she was old.

10. *No, it doesn't say she was old. Do you think it would be all right if she was old?*
You said she was an old lady.

11. *No, I just said his wife.*
If she was real old I guess it would be okay . . .

12. *Why would it be okay?*
Well, couldn't he get the money?

13. *He couldn't. He tried everything. There just wasn't anymore money that anyone could let him have.*
Why didn't he have something in his bank?

14. *He took all the money out of his bank. There just wasn't anymore. So he either had to steal the drug or his wife would die. And she wasn't very old, I don't think. It doesn't say she was old.*
Well, let's see.

15. *Do you still think that it's worse to steal than to let his wife die?*
Even his best friends wouldn't give him any money?

16. *His best friends were all poor, I guess, because . . .*
Well . . .

17. *Have you made up your mind?*
I decided that he shouldn't have stealed the drug.

18. *Why not?*
Because that would be bad, stealing.

19. *Why?*
Wait a minute. I think I changed my mind . . . ummmmm . . . I think if he didn't then his wife would die . . . she would be dead . . . he wouldn't want his wife dead.

20. *Why wouldn't he want her dead?*
Because she was his wife and he probably loved her.

21. *What if he didn't love her? Should he still steal the drug?*
No . . . Yes, I told you he should.

22. *Why should he do it if he doesn't love her?*
    Well, do you want to save a life or not?

23. *If he didn't like her anymore, would he still want to save her life?*
    Yeah.

24. *Why do you think that?*
    Because . . . ummmmm . . . it's another person's life, and you should always save a person's life.

25. *Why do you think a person's life is important?*
    'Cause that's the only life they have and stuff, and a drug isn't a life.

26. *Why is a life more important than a drug?*
    Because . . . ummmmm . . . a life's a life.

27. *And what's a drug?*
    It's something that helps you get better.

28. *What if it was his dog or cat who is very sick? Should he steal it for a pet dog or cat?*
    No.

29. *Why not?*
    Because a dog or cat isn't as important as a life of a human being.

30. *Why is the life of a human being more important?*
    Because . . . 'cause it's a person.

31. *Why is a person more important? Can you think of any reason?*
    No, I can't, and it's really hard.

32. *I know it's hard. It really makes you think.*
    You can always buy another dog or cat, but you can't buy another you or something.

Note the importance of the why questions in this interview. At any stage, stealing can be considered wrong and human life important. Therefore, it is necessary to find out why, and then the reasons given will begin to indicate structure.

Stage structure is determined by means of a scoring manual which Kohlberg and his associates have produced. For the Heinz dilemma, the manual is divided into two sections. One section contains characteristic reasons given to support obedience to the law. In looking through the descriptions in the manual we find the following:

> Heinz or one should not steal because it belongs to the druggist, and Heinz should not take it from him; OR because it's the druggist's property to do what he wants; OR because he worked for it or invented it and it's his; . . .

And under this general description we find the following example:

> *Why is it not right to steal?*
> "That's taking someone else's property, that's not yours. It's their property they've gotten it, probably worked for it, and it's theirs."[7]

This answer is listed as Stage 2. Comparing it with Janie's answer to question 4, we find we have a good match, and Janie's answer is scored as Stage 2.

The second section of the manual gives reasons to support stealing the drug. We find the following description and example in the manual:

> "Heinz should steal the drug because his wife needs it or will die without it; OR because he wants her to live; . . .
>
> *Should Heinz Steal the Drug?*
> "Yes, if he loves his wife, he should do whatever he can to save her.
> *Why?* Or else she'll die."[8]

This answer is listed as Stage 2 and since Janie's responses to questions 19 and 20 are a good match, they are scored as Stage 2.

Scoring requires a great deal of discipline and practice in order to avoid reading the scorer's own understandings and structure into the answers. In responsible research, two or more individuals score the same interview and then hold a scoring conference to compare results. A scoring conference is a strong corrective for beginning scorers and a constant check on the work of the experienced.

A person's score for each issue, e.g. law and life, and for the total interview is determined by careful procedures.

Scoring for moral reasoning brings together four major elements. The first consists of the two conflicting issues presented by the particular dilemma. These are inherent in the dilemma and the particular questions asked, and are external to the person responding. In trying to solve the conflict between the two issues, however, individuals ordinarily choose one of the two (an internal choice) and focus on it in their reasoning or bring in another issue to support it. For instance, in question 4, Janie supported the law issue by bringing in the issue of property. Whatever issue is spontaneously used by a person is considered to be the second element and is called a "norm." The norms are the values used by a subject when supporting or justifying his or her choice of issues.

The third element consists of the modes or strategies used by persons of any stage in making moral decisions. The four modes are:

1) The using of standards or rules.
2) Looking at consequences or results.
3) Considering what is fair among persons. This involves justice and respect for personal autonomy and dignity.
4) Considering what a good person would do in terms of obeying one's conscience, maintaining self-respect, and living up to moral law.

These modes are built into the methodology found in the Scoring Manual.

The fourth element in scoring for moral reasoning is, of course, the stage of social perspective. It is the combination of norms, modes, and social perspective in response to the dilemma issues that provides the basis for the individual's moral reasoning and produces the data for scoring.

A numerical score in moral reasoning describes the

percentage of times a stage or stages were used in a particular series of interviews. For instance, a score of 1(2) means that the subject used Stage 1 reasoning in more than 50 percent of the statements scored, with the remainder scored as Stage 2. A score of 2 indicates that the subject's reasoning was over 80 percent at Stage 2. In our research, most people have scored at mixed stages.

Another method for assessing moral judgment stages is the Defining Issues Test (DIT) constructed by James Rest and colleagues. This test

attempts to assess what people see as crucial moral issues in a situation by presenting subjects with a moral dilemma and a list of definitions of the major issues involved. In the case of Heinz's dilemma of whether to steal the drug, for example, subjects have been asked to consider such issues as "whether or not a community's laws are going to be upheld," and "Isn't it only natural for a loving husband to care so much for his wife that he'd steal?"[9]

It is an attempt to assess moral judgment using an objective format. This test usually taps the highest level of moral reasoning that a person can understand, rather than eliciting the reasoning actually utilized, as Kohlberg's open-ended interview tries to do.

Kohlberg is unique among contemporary psychologists in using philosophy as a basis for defining what is moral. His developmental theory is based on the principle of justice. He sees the most integrated and differentiated concept of justice as the end point in the development of moral reasoning. So, Kohlberg argues, if one can scientifically observe and describe individuals developing more complex concepts of justice as they become more integrated and differentiated, then one can logically move to the idea that such development is what ought to be ("is to ought").

Kohlberg has been critiqued extensively about his use of one philosophical category and his "is to ought" statements. It is not within the scope of this book to explore all the questions which have been raised about structural developmental theory and about Kohlberg's model in particular. But it would be irresponsible to fail to mention that legitimate questions have been raised, and to suggest further readings in this area.[10] On the other hand, some of the criticism which has been leveled at developmental theory is irresponsible in that the writers show a serious lack of understanding of the theories which they critique. It is important to distinguish the latter from the challenges which should be considered.

I will now introduce the fourth strand in current developmental theory, the faith development model of James W. Fowler. Fowler's model received its original impetus from the results of his many interviews with persons about the significant experiences in their lives. Subsequently, it has been expanded and informed by the work of Piaget, Kohlberg, Erikson, Selman, Kegan, and others. To encompass this fourth strand in human development, Fowler uses the term "faithing" as a verb describing a universal mode of relating to what he calls our "ultimate environment." In this broad usage the term "faithing" may or may not be related to any formal belief or religion.

Fowler describes six stages which generally parallel those of Kohlberg. The chart, "Four Cognitive Structural Developmental Models," lists the divisions of each of the four strands or models and enables the reader to see similarities and differences. Instead of moral issues or factors of social perspective, Fowler describes seven "aspects" of faith development. Some of these will be familiar to the reader: authority and role-taking (from social perspective), logical reasoning (Piaget's model), and moral judgment (Kohlberg's model). His aspect, "bounds of social awareness," closely parallels the factor of society and community used in social perspective. A sixth aspect, "form of world-coherence," introduces some new ideas, and a seventh, "role of symbols," is a completely new addition to structural developmental

FOUR COGNITIVE STRUCTURAL DEVELOPMENTAL MODELS

Logical Reasoning (Piaget) "Operations"	Social Perspective (Wilcox) "Factors"	Moral Reasoning (Kohlberg) "Issues"	Faith (Fowler) "Aspects"
Seriation	Law	Laws and rules	Bounds of social awareness
Conservation	Value of (human) life	Conscience	Authority
Classification	Society	Personal roles of affection	Role-taking
Logical addition and multiplication	Authority	Authority	Moral judgment (Kohlberg)
Reversibility	Role-taking	Civil rights	Form of logic (Piaget)
Decentration	Persons	Contract, trust, and justice in exchange	Role of symbols
Perspective-taking		Punishment and justice	World-coherence
		The value of life	
		Property rights and values	
		Truth	
		Sex and sexual love	

All of the above can be looked at from the standpoint of variable degrees of complexity, differentiation, integration, and equilibration. The degree of variation is described by "stages," "periods," or "levels."

theory. In faithing Fowler says that we are involved in relating ourselves to the realities of our environment and daily lives and that the relationship can only be represented through symbols, rituals, myths, or metaphors.[11] The flag is an example of a growing symbolic function. At Stage 1, it is simply a piece of colorful cloth on a stick, although it may be perceived in highly imaginative ways. At Stage 2, it may stand for national holidays or other concrete experience. It is only at later stages that it becomes symbolic of deeper and more abstract meanings.

In the same way, a Stage 1 concept of the Bible may be simply that of a big book, perhaps with magical qualities, such qualities having been derived from exposure to adult attitudes. At Stage 2, it may be a book of stories about Jesus. But whether we are talking about the flag or the Bible, we are dealing wih symbols which mediate meaning, and how meaning is understood is based on the way the structural stage filters and shapes the content of particular ideas.

Fowler's model of faith development encompasses the other three models with unique contributions of its own. Some aspects of his theory directly relate to the functioning of the mind in its metaphorical and imaginative operations. Fowler's focus on symbol informs us how persons at different stages may appropriate the symbols of community, nation, culture, or religion. And since the values of such entities are communicated in large part through the use of symbols, this opens up new vistas or suggests new methods in various areas of education.

In concluding this chapter, I want to make a point that is critically important in our use of developmental theory. We need to be particularly attentive that we do not oversimplify nor make snap impressionistic judgments in using these theories, thereby doing great injustice to both the theories and to individual persons. A developmental model can give us clues about human potential and ways of facilitating its achievement. It can provide a basis for more effective interpersonal relationships and communication, for educational goals, methods, and learning skills, and for decision-making. But its responsible use does not permit labeling or trying to mold persons to fit into the contours of the model, nor does it justify ignoring other aspects of the personality. But it can open up new vistas.

In the next chapter we return to descriptions of how people think and interpret their worlds.

Developmental Journey

QUIZ

Column A	Column B
1. The normal growing organism tends to become increasingly_____	1. role of symbols
2. A cognitive stage is a consistent_____	2. complex and differentiated and integrated
3. Stages are hierarchical, invariant, and _____	3. a great deal of discipline and practice
4. Cognitive conflict means _____	4. four major factors
5. Structure is most likely to be elicited through the use of questions of _____	5. should and why
6. Scoring requires _____	6. inconsistencies and contradictions in one's thinking
7. Scoring for moral reasoning brings together _____	7. pattern of thinking, a structured whole
8. Fowler's faith development model introduces the aspect of _____	8. universal

ANSWERS

1. 2   2. 7   3. 8   4. 6   5. 5   6. 3   7. 4   8. 1

CHAPTER V
Thinking Takes Wings

INTRODUCTION

The preoperational child—the child of wonder—is not inhibited by logical and lawful constraints and freely explores the world through imagination and flights of fancy. The bookkeeper, the person who is concrete-operational, works industriously at making logical sense out of the world, at organizing and classifying. The person using formal operations combines qualities from each of the earlier periods: the need for a solid foundation of logic and order augmented by the ability to soar beyond this into possibilities of what might be.

I have previously described how children who are preoperational and concrete-operational in their thinking arrange straws of varying lengths in a series. Now I suggest that you try this problem mentally: If Stick A is longer than Stick B and shorter than Stick C, which stick is the shortest?

Many adults find this a challenging task. Some will say, "I formed a picture of the sticks in my mind." Others will work it out with mathematical symbols. Some take pencil and paper and draw the sticks. Yet this question is simply another way of presenting the simple seriation of sticks.

Why is this problem so much more difficult than the earlier examples? Because it is presented solely by means of words and requires mental operations which have no concrete referent, no actual sticks to arrange. It is an example of a simple form of abstract thinking; Piaget describes such thinking as the *Period of Formal Operations*. In this chapter we will begin to explore the implications of formal operations for the construction of a social world and for the making of moral decisions at

Viewpoints ("Windows")	Divisions	Periods . . . Levels/Stages						
Moral Reasoning	Issues Life Law etc.	Stage 0		**Preconventional Level**		**Conventional Level**		**Postconventional Level**
				Stage 1	Stage 2	Stage 3	Stage 4	Stage 5
Social Perspective	Factors Authority Law etc.	Stage 0		**Preconventional Level**		**Conventional Level**		**Postconventional Level**
				Stage 1	Stage 2	Stage 3	Stage 4	Stage 5
Logical Reasoning	Operations Conservation Seriation Reversibility etc.	Sensorimotor Period Age 0-1½	Preoperational Period Age 1½-7	Period of Concrete Operations Age 6 ⟶		Period of Formal Operations Age 11 ⟶		

Figure 1

higher stages. Relationships among the periods, levels, and stages are shown in figure 1.

LOGICAL REASONING: THE PERIOD OF FORMAL OPERATIONS

Formal operations involve the same basic operations as concrete operations, such as conservation, seriation, and classification. But now the operations are performed on verbal descriptions and abstractions and can evolve into the formation of hypotheses. This means that the person must "reflect on these operations in the absence of the objects, which are replaced by pure propositions."[1] It means that thinking is independent of concrete reality, that "thinking takes wings," as Piaget has said.

Formal operational thinking becomes a possibility for persons moving toward adolescence, but this does not mean that all adolescents accomplish it. One set of tests given to a group of college freshmen at a university in Oklahoma showed that 50 percent of the subjects were concrete thinkers, 25 percent were moving into formal operations, and 25 percent were fully formal-operational.[2]

In a study of lower- and upper-middle class families, 45 percent of persons age ten to fifteen were able to do formal-operational thinking, as were 53 percent of those age sixteen to twenty, 65 percent of those age twenty-one to thirty, and 57 percent of those aged forty-five to fifty.[3] These results are based on the accomplishment of one task. In the same study another task was completed satisfactorily by even fewer members of the adult population. As with development from preoperational thinking to concrete operations, the movement from concrete to formal thinking tends to occur one step at a time as the individual accomplishes different tasks. It seems apparent, however, that many adults achieve few of the tasks related to formal operations.

I am now going to describe two problems to demonstrate formal operational thinking. One of the characteristics of such thinking is the ability to entertain all possible solutions of a problem and include all possible combinations of the elements. The following example demonstrates this characteristic.

COMBINING CHEMICAL SUBSTANCES [4]

Materials:
- —four flasks containing four chemically different clear liquids numbered 1, 2, 3, and 4
- —a bottle with dropper containing clear liquid (this fifth liquid is labelled "g")
- —a glass containing 1 + 3
- —a glass containing 2 (See figure 2)

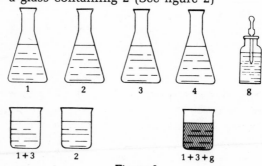

Figure 2

Experiment:
1. The experimenter adds g to 1 + 3, and the liquid turns yellow.
2. The experimenter adds g to 2, and there is no change.
3. The child is asked to duplicate the yellow color by combining the liquids in any way he or she chooses.

Description of how subjects responded:

Preoperational children combined liquids at random. If they accidentally created the yellow liquid, their explanations tended to be magically oriented, and they were unable to duplicate the experiment.

Concrete operational children combined g with each of the liquids 1, 2, 3, and 4, but were unable to go beyond this dyadic combination systematically. Beyond that their attempts were random, and if the yellow color resulted, they were unable to duplicate the procedure.

Formal operational subjects systematically worked through the possibilities and were able to explain what they were doing and why.

In these last subjects, who were at the formal operational level, we see the operation of a whole combinatorial system based on a cognitive structure "in the head."

The second problem relates to the construction of systems and appears to be a crucial concept in the development of higher levels of social perspective. This problem again involves the use of sticks, but note that there is a difference between this question and the seriation question.

Problem: If Stick A is longer than Stick B, and Stick B is shorter than Stick C, which is the shortest and what is the relationship among the three? (figure 3).

All we can ascertain from the problem is that Stick B is the shortest of the three. We cannot tell which of the other two is longer or whether they are the same length. Sticks A and C have an unknown relationship to one another, but both relate in the same way to Stick B, both being longer than Stick B. Therefore, we have two objects related to one another only through a third object, thus forming a triadic (three-way) system (figure 4). The significance of this particular formal operation for social perspective will be explored in the next chapter which describes Stage 4.

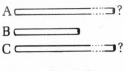

Figure 3

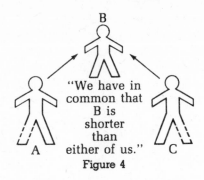

Figure 4

Another formal operation that is critical for the development of social perspective is the ability to stand outside of oneself and see the self and another person from a third-person viewpoint. This allows one to anticipate what another person might be thinking and feeling, and in addition, to know that the other is also able to anticipate what the self is thinking and feeling.

Formal operations signify the ability to think abstractly, to form hypotheses, to theorize, to imagine many possibilities and combinations, to generate multiple solutions to problems, to comprehend subtle and symbolic meanings, and to perform operations in the mind by mentally manipulating objects without the objects being present. It means to be able to "think about thinking," to reflect upon one's own thought processes, to stand back and observe them objectively. It means combining operations into whole systems of operations. Formal operations "might be impressionistically characterized as a sort of mental scaffolding held up by a number of girders joined to each other in such a way that an agile subject can always get from any point—vertically or horizontally—to any other without trapping himself in a dead end."[5]

Structural theory of development implies that it is the greater complexity and differentiation of the structure of thinking at each subsequent level that makes possible the processing of data in increasingly complex ways. Piaget's study of thinking did not go beyond that of adolescence, and little has been done toward studying adult reasoning. Three scientists who have recently produced intriguing descriptions of logical thinking in adulthood are James W. Fowler, Herbert Koplowitz, and William G. Perry.

Fowler, in his research on faith development, has proposed styles of formal operations used by adults which he relates to stages of faithing.[6] Based on his brief definitions, I have expanded his ideas into the following descriptions.

The first style in the series is *compartmentalization*, in which opposing views exist side-by-side but generally are considered separately. One of my students suggested a way of depicting compartmentalization and the other styles, which I use here.[7]

Imagine that you are standing with your arms stretched out on either side. Your hands each represent values or views which are in opposition to one another (figure 5). Obviously, you can look in only one direction at a time and can see only one idea at a time. The opposing idea is out of sight, blocked out. This describes how the mind compartmentalizes. For example, the ability to uphold one type of ethics in personal life and another in business, without experiencing conflict and tension, is probably cognitive compartmentalization.

compartmentalization   dichotomizing
                                either/or

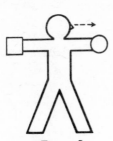

Figure 5   Figure 6

Now bring both of your arms out in front of you. Your hands are both visible and you can see the conflict between opposing ideas (figure 6). The conflict may stimulate the cognitive function of *dichotomizing*, meaning to cut or divide into two (or more) parts those things which are opposed to one another by contradictions. Continuing with the example, the person with opposing ethical standards can now see the conflict and may be forced to choose either one or the other. We can also illustrate this style by taking the person who is a "liberal" politically or religiously and who sees "conservatives" as standing for a conflicting view that cannot be reconciled to his or her own view. To dichotomize means to make an either/or choice. In formal operations, this means the ability to make such a choice between conflicting value *systems*, not merely between concrete objects or simple ideas.

Now look again at those two hands out in front of you. Suppose that you see that there might be value in each idea, you would then be developing a style which is *dialectical* rather than dichotomizing. Dialectical means weighing and reconciling contradictory arguments, seeking to resolve the conflict between opposing ideas. This is depicted in figure 7.

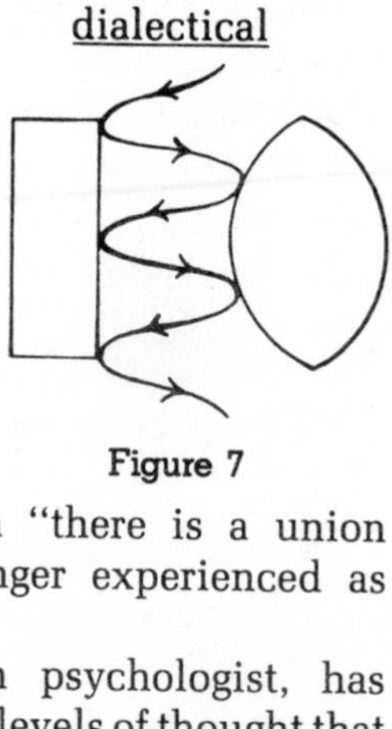

dialectical

Figure 7

Fowler describes a further style, that of synthesis, in which "there is a union of the opposites which is no longer experienced as paradoxical."[8]

Herbert Koplowitz, a Canadian psychologist, has recently proposed that there are two levels of thought that transcend Piaget's Formal Operations. He describes Formal Operations as characterized by conventional scientific thought in which variables are separated out from a whole. This mode is followed by his Systems level in which variables are perceived as interdependent parts of a whole and ultimately nonseparable. Finally, at the highest level, Unitary Operational Thought, the individual's understanding of his or her perception of how the world is constructed is recognized as only one of many possible constructions or organizations of experience.[9]

William G. Perry conducted studies among students at Harvard University during the 1950s and early 1960s.[10] He describes nine "positions" that are in part descriptions of logical reasoning at the level of formal operations. The first four positions are oriented toward a world-view of absolute truths with either blind conformity to these absolutes or equally blind revolt against them. Diverse points of view are perceived as discrete and irreconcilable, but may be accepted on the basis that "anyone has a right to his or her own opinion."

A transitional fifth position describes a transformation in orientation to a world-view which is perceived as basically relativistic. The remaining four positions represent increasing ability to consider diverse points of view through analysis, comparison, and evaluation, with the development of autonomous commitments.

I am presently working with this model in ongoing research and find it very informative.

Persons who function regularly with formal operations have described the processes by which they concretize concepts in order to comprehend them more adequately. They often accomplish this through the formation of mental pictures and the construction of diagrams and models like some of the diagrammatic illustrations in this book which have been used to concretely represent ideas. From my research, it appears that when people lose the ability to concretize they have difficulty relating abstract theory to concrete situations. This may result from lack of practice in making such connections, due to remaining at the abstract level. It is an important area for further investigation and raises critical questions for the educational process.

Piaget stresses the implications of the structure of formal operations for affective (emotional) situations as well. He says: "The change of perspective is as important for affective as for cognitive development, for the world of values also can remain bound by concrete and perceptible reality, or it can encompass many interpersonal and social possibilities."[11]

The intention of this section on formal operations has been to open some windows through which we may view the journey of persons along the path of logical reasoning. The ever-widening circles of clearing in the jungle, through which that path runs, open up new possibilities for the journey in social perspective and moral reasoning.

SOCIAL PERSPECTIVE

With the beginning of formal operations and the potential for soaring into new realms of thinking, the development of a Stage 3 social perspective becomes a possibility. There is now some ability to think about thinking, to form hypotheses beyond those operations which depend on concrete experiences, and—of great importance—to construct relationships based on continuity and affection.

CONVENTIONAL LEVEL: STAGE 3

Concepts of Law

What is the law? What is its purpose or function?

"A good law is one that does a majority of good as it's intended to do."

"Laws should only be made so they let people grow more fully."

"Some laws are better than others because they fit good behavior, they allow you to be as good a person as you can be."

These statements are not concerned with the concrete destructive acts of Stage 2, but rather depict the purpose of law as supportive of good behavior and personal growth. Good behavior may include compassion and caring. At Stage 3, laws might be described as guidelines for good behavior and the prevention of chaos. Breaking the law may be justified if it is for a good cause such as helping somebody or making something good happen. Note the relationship between law and good intentions.

Value of Human Life

Which is more important or of more value, a person or a pet?

"Human life is more important or more valuable than anything; people feel a greater sense of loss if a person dies, compared with the death of a pet."

"All life is equally valuable. Some people love their pets like people."

"I figure a pet has got as much right to live as anybody else; maybe the owner goes for animals."

In these responses there are two different conclusions: (1) human life is more valuable than animal life, (2) all life is equally valuable. These are differences in content. The structure that underlies these conclusions is: the value of life depends primarily on *how people feel about it*, on how much people love a particular animal or person. This is the keyhole that shapes the input into conclusions. The concept of usefulness found at Stage 2 has disappeared as the structural criterion for the valuing of human life. At Stage 3, something new appears which we have not yet seen on this journey: love and relationships of affection. This has as its basis logical abilities related to role-taking and a perception of continuity which now extends beyond concrete experience. These two features are described in the next two factors.

Role-Taking Ability

I have used the example of the mountains and the little doll to demonstrate role-taking in a physical, perceptual sense. Advanced concrete operations allow a person to consistently put the self in the position of the little doll and to correctly predict the view that the doll sees. There are other tests that measure the ability to anticipate what another person might be thinking and feeling. In addition, there is the understanding that another person is able to anticipate what the self is thinking and feeling. This can take place simultaneously and mutually and is what Robert Selman calls "reciprocal or mutual role-taking."[12] It is as if one can take the position of a third person observing the self and another as they engage in the process of role-taking.

Stage 3 role-taking involves the kind of reversibility expressed in the Golden Rule: "Always treat others as you would like them to treat you."[13] The difficulty of achieving this concept is demonstrated by a quotation from a ten-year-old: "Well, it's like your brain has to leave your head and go into the other guy's head and then come back into your head but you still see it like it was in the other guy's head and then you decide that way."[14]

Stage 3 role-taking involves empathy, the ability to project oneself into the feelings and ideas of another. It tends to be limited, however, by the inability to put the self in the place of another whose values are substantially different from one's own. (For this reason it is called "first-order role-taking" to distinguish it from Stage 6 "ideal role-taking.") As an example, parents with deep roots in a particular religious tradition may be unable to put themselves in the role of a son or daughter who has embraced a radically different religion, and who in turn is unable to identify with the concern of the parents.

Concepts of Persons

The following is a question we asked interviewees about the Heinz dilemma and one of their responses.

Q: Would it be as right to steal for a stranger or for a wife Heinz didn't love as for someone he loved?

A: Yes, he must have loved his wife once, just the past would be a good enough reason to steal.

Compare this answer with one given from a Stage 2 perspective: "If he didn't love his wife he probably wouldn't do it for her and would want her to die . . . but she's a person and maybe he'd start liking her again."

In the Stage 3 response we see a new aspect of thinking: the ability to understand the intrinsic value of a stable and continuing relationship based on sentiment and affection rather than on usefulness and "on again/off again" relationships seen at Stage 2. Heinz should steal for his wife on the basis of love, whether past or present (continuity), and not because "he needs her," as at Stage 2. However, at Stage 3 the decision *not* to steal may be made on the basis of lack of *emotional* motivation: "I don't see why he'd steal if he doesn't love her." This is still a two-way relationship (dyadic), but it is empathetic dyadic because it involves relating to the feelings and thoughts of another rather than to the person's usefulness.

The ability to form such relationships means that for the first time on the developmental journey a person looks at the world from a point of view that is jointly shared with and defined by others. These others are those with whom one has immediate, concrete relationships of affection: family, close friends, members of the groups to which one belongs, upon which one depends for approval, and cues as to what is right and wrong. It is natural and right to value these persons more than others, to be more concerned for them than for mere acquaintances or strangers: "Yes, I'd steal for my husband. But whether I'd steal for a friend depends on the degree of friendship." The desire to maintain positive personal relationships creates a strong concern for approval. Doing wrong can result in losing face and shame before one's family and/or friends. However, good intentions, which are recognized at Stage 2, are highly valued at Stage 3. One's failure to do the right thing can be understood and excused if one's intentions were good.

107

When the child or adult with Stage 3 perspective extends concern to persons outside his or her affectional group, it is likely to be limited to those who are perceived as weaker or less fortunate. This kind of concern provides the object for good intentions and simple concrete responses to "the poor," "the hungry," and others in unfortunate situations. Sometimes, such a response is highly appropriate and may be appreciated by its recipients. But when it is not, there is little cognitive ability at Stage 3 to determine why it is not received with gratitude. Subtle needs such as the maintenance of self-respect are not easily perceived through Stage 3 role-taking. The structure does not allow ready processing of viewpoints radically different from one's own, or of complex sociological and political factors. In a concern for the alleviation of world hunger, some organizations are trying to identify and respond to the complicated underlying causes. A common response to their approach is: "Let's not worry about all that. Why don't we just collect food? People understand that." This seems to express a Stage 3 social perspective.

A limitation is that the self and others are seen in stereotypical images. What people learn from close, concretely experienced groups defines what they see as "good and bad" behavior and roles. For instance, a "good" wife may be one who stays home and takes care of the family and pleases her husband. Yet in another person's experience, a "good" wife may be one who asserts her own identity and espouses the movement for women's rights. Such definitions tend to be simple and unable to encompass complexities and opposing points of view.

Archie Bunker in the television program, *All in the Family*, has expressed the traditional stereotypes of minorities and other groups who don't conform to Archie's conventional standards. In a climate in which support of civil rights has become "a good thing," Archie's attitudes have become less acceptable. But in reaction to such attitudes new stereotypes have emerged. Love, tolerance, and relativism are pervasive stereotypes in our present culture and suggest images of universal caring. "Helping your fellow man is a good thing. You should show concern for any other person, it doesn't matter who he is." "Every person isn't responsible for himself, he's responsible for helping other people and . . . giving away, by giving you receive, and you're not all wrapped up in yourself." But at Stage 3 this concern may not extend to people who are intolerant or who do not help others. What is considered a "good" behavior or role is different, but whatever the content of the image, that particular stereotype will be projected on others. The *structure* in stereotyping is the keyhole that shapes a Stage 3 concept of persons; the *content* of the stereotypes varies according to the culture, subculture, or significant group.

Concepts of Authority

Authorities are no longer seen as omnipotent, as at Stage 1, or as self-serving, but personally respected, as at Stage 2. Stage 3 requires that authorities have admirable personal qualities and some sanctioning from one's group or culture or from respected institutions. The role of authority, in itself, confers positive qualities on the persons who fill this role. They are often seen as benevolent, helpful, and understanding of the problems of others. For instance, the role of president of the United States implies that the person who fills that role has certain admirable qualities. When an individual fails to live up to those characteristics, conflict is created in Stage 3 structure, and there is difficulty in accepting the contradictions. Many persons continued to disbelieve the information generated by Watergate because it did not jibe with their idea of the role of the president.

When a person runs into conflicting behaviors or roles in relationships with authority, either as individuals or as valued affectional groups, the cognitive conflict is resolved through compartmentalization (explained in the previous section on logical reasoning) or through prioritizing. In compartmentalization, opposing views exist side-by-side and generally are considered separately. "At school, it is all right to cheat because everybody does it. At home, it's not all right because my parents would get upset." Or compartmentalization might involve one set of ethics for business and another for home or religion. The contradictions are not perceived or are accepted on the assumption that there are certain things that don't make sense so "let it be."

In prioritizing, one person or group takes precedence over others and determines the values of the individual. A meaningful religious relationship may furnish the basis of authority or it may be parents and family or friends or the corporation that provides one's security.

Therefore, note that authority is external, it lies primarily outside the person, and is generally tacitly assumed, although there may be some sense of having chosen between authorities. For instance, during adolescence when Stage 3 social perspective is common, there is a shift in respect for the authority of parents to the authority of teachers, leaders, or peer group. The young person may be aware of this shift, but may not recognize that his or her values are still external and determined by others.

Concepts of Society

A Stage 3 concept of society begins with the dyadic empathetic structure (two-way identification with others). Affectional groups or communities are the structure of society, with laws functioning as guidelines for appropriate behavior. The values of one's own group are perceived as facts of life, not as self-chosen options, and feelings figure strongly in one's commitments. One's values are accepted as "truth." Joseph Pearce made this statement about such fundamental assumptions: "People do not know that they are tacitly assuming, for no other way of putting things has ever occurred to them; they are always merely responding to 'obvious facts.' "[15]

In some ways this can be true for all stages, but it is especially appropriate as a description of a Stage 3 orientation to one's culture and society.

However, this is the first stage in the developmental journey in which social perspective includes a *community* of persons, and this community determines the values and commitments one holds. At Stage 3, one can identify on a feeling level with individuals who are outside of one's own group, but to "get inside" the world-view of a community with differing values is not yet possible. Communities are perceived as discrete objects, separated from one another and without the overarching structures which function at Stage 4.

MORAL REASONING

CONVENTIONAL LEVEL: STAGE 3

At Stage 3, the stereotypical images of good behavior determined by one's own group are a primary basis of moral reasoning. "Right" is conformity to these images in order to avoid the disapproval of others.

The justice structure is a first-order application of the Golden Rule. The "others," mentioned in the Golden Rule, are the good or deserving who are in need of help. The self is seen as one who initiates or offers help and the recipient as one who responds with gratitude. Helping is right because "It makes me feel good," "It is a good thing to do." The definition of who needs help is embedded in what Kohlberg calls a "bag of virtues and role stereotypes." Justice is seen as the right of "good" persons to receive better treatment than those who don't fit one's stereotype of good.

For example, several years ago the United Presbyterian Church in the U.S.A. appropriated funds for the defense trial of Angela Davis, a black woman and avowed Communist who was charged as an accomplice in a

California courthouse shootout. Many local church congregations were highly incensed by the action of the national church body, and there were demands that the decision be reversed. A commonly expressed reason for this demand was that "Angela Davis is a Communist and doesn't deserve a fair trial."

One man who made such a statement subsequently participated in a study in which he was exposed to the negative experiences of several black persons with the court system. In a complete reversal of his previous position, he subsequently concluded: "She is a black person and therefore won't get a fair trial, so she should be given the money. It's a Christian thing to do." His personal contact with persons who had been treated unjustly changed his stereotypes of both the courts and of black persons, and both decisions appear to be the result of moral reasoning based on stereotypical images.

Good intentions are another major factor in Stage 3 moral reasoning and may justify otherwise questionable actions.

> "I don't think Heinz should have stolen the drug . . . though it's not that terribly bad of an act because it was done in hope of helping someone. The druggist was really the cause of the stealing because he was too wrapped up in himself."

> "I think it's all right to tell a lie to save hurt feelings. Sometimes, it might be better to tell a lie. It's awfully hard if someone has a brand new dress and they say, 'How do you like my dress?' and you just don't like it at all. It wouldn't be kind to say, 'I think it's ugly.' "

In these examples we see not only the function of good intentions in making moral decisions, but expressions of empathy—not hurting feelings, doing the kind thing. Empathy is a quality of social perspective from Stage 3 on, but at stage 3 its feeling aspect tends to dominate moral decision-making to the exclusion of other considerations. Therefore, it is not surprising that at Stage 3 conscience and guilt seem to be related to feelings of shame, disapproval by others, and "losing face" with family and friends, as well as with strangers. Breaking a promise may be considered wrong because of what "other people would think of me."

Loyalty to friends and superiors is a basis for moral decision-making. Herbert Porter, the Watergate participant quoted at the opening of chapter 1, explained his illegal actions in the affair on the basis of loyalty to Richard Nixon. The Stage 3 concept of authority plays an important part in this, because authority figures are seen as good, competent, intelligent, benevolent. In another example, Lt. Calley, who took part in the slaughter of civilians at Mylai, explained why he shot them:

> Because that's what I was instructed to do, Sir, and I had delayed long enough. I was trying to get out of there before I got criticized again. . . . I was a run-of-the-mill average guy. I still am. I always said the people in Washington are smarter than me. If intelligent people say Communism is bad, it's going to engulf us (sic). I was only a Second Lieutenant. I had to obey and hope that the people in Washington were smarter than me.[16]

Another young man, a conscientious objector, used the same structure of reasoning, and came to a different conclusion about war because he appealed to different sources of authority. He explained his stand in terms of his parents' teachings that war was wrong, and the teachings of his church and of Jesus that we should not kill, but love one another.

These examples demonstrate once again that structure is not made visible through conclusions, but rather through reasons and social perspective. Answers to *Should Heinz steal the drug and why?* show this also:

Pro

—Yes, because letting someone die is more wrong than stealing. The life of the wife was more worthy than the greediness of the druggist.

—Yes, you should be concerned for the life of everyone.
—Yes, helping someone stay alive is a good thing.
(In the last two examples, affection is extended and
    generalized to all persons.)

Con

—No, I wouldn't want to make other people, the druggist,
    feel badly.
—No, because he'd be taking from someone else. They
    should sit down and plan how they would make the
    most out of the situation, how we can teach others from
    it. And in that way the wife would be giving as much as
    she could from her death and therefore it would be
    worthwhile.

Decisions made on the basis of Stage 3 compassionate
models and stereotypes can result in highly altruistic and
satisfying life-styles. But these models may fail as
adequate sources of moral reasoning when there are
conflicts within them or among competing stereotypes.
For example, a college student responded to the Heinz
dilemma in terms of her commitment to the idea of
"giving" as opposed to "taking."

> Ideally what would be good for everyone is if everybody gives
> and everybody receives, sort of a cycle of giving and receiving.
> When you say "give me," just grabbing, it disrupts that
> cycle. . . . Heinz was taking from someone else, violently
> taking from the drug store. He and his wife were really
> thinking of themselves. He was worried about his wife, he's
> not looking any farther than that. . . . They should plan how
> they can teach others from it, and in that way even though she
> died she'd be giving by her death and that would be
> worthwhile.

When it was pointed out to this young woman that
"taking" the drug might be Heinz's way of "giving" to his
wife, giving her life, she was thrown into real cognitive
conflict. She said repeatedly, "I never thought of that.

That's weird." She became aware of contradictions within her stereotype of "giving and taking." It is such conflict that stimulates an individual toward ways of moral reasoning which more adequately resolve the tensions.

SUMMARY OF STAGE 3

The great step forward for Stage 3 is in role-taking and in understanding stable interpersonal relationships, with a resulting sense of community. This is still primarily tacit and unself-conscious.

In the use of symbols as described by Fowler, the symbol is no longer linked solely to a concrete object, but may have a variety of meanings including the metaphorical. The Bible is not simply a book of stories, but becomes a guidebook offering examples for good and loving attitudes, for whatever content has been learned by the individual. The flag also represents more abstract meanings—love of country, in some cases, or support for war, in others—the images will be positive or negative again depending on the content that has been learned and experienced. Images and meanings are less concrete than at Stage 2. At Stage 3, the symbol no longer requires a concrete referent, but it is still bound to the meaning it symbolizes and cannot be separated from it. So a desecration of the Bible or of the flag is perceived as a desecration of the meaning it symbolizes.

The major limitations of Stage 3 arise from the inconsistencies which are externally determined and come from several sources of authority. There is an awareness of one's values, but the relationships among them cannot be clearly reflected upon and sorted out. A Stage 3 social perspective lacks clarity and contains much that is conflicting or simply not understandable. Many people are comfortable in such a world. But for the individual who is not, Stage 4 provides a structure for resolving some of the tensions.

Stage 3 is the first step in the broad level which Kohlberg calls **Conventional.** The movement toward Stage 4 (the second stage in the **Conventional Level**) can be seen as an expansion of one's concept of community/ society and therefore an expansion of the sources of one's values.

QUIZ

Here is a brief review quiz for chapter 5. Match the statements in Column A with their completions in Column B.

Column A	*Column B*
1. In formal operations, such operations as seriation are performed on _____	1. dichotomizing.
2. A whole combinatorial system "in the head" is an example of _____	2. stable and continuing relationships of affection.
3. When contradictory ideas can be understood but not reconciled or brought into dialogue, this is called _____	3. verbal descriptions and abstractions in the absence of concrete objects.
4. At Stage 3, breaking the law can be justified if it means _____	4. stereotypical images of good behavior.
5. A significant new element found at Stage 3 is the ability to understand _____	5. formal operations.
6. Stage 3 understanding of symbols is no longer tied to _____	6. helping somebody, or if the intentions are good.
7. A major source of moral reasoning at Stage 3 is _____	7. concrete objects.

ANSWERS
1. 3   2. 5   3. 1   4. 6   5. 2   6. 7   7. 4

CHAPTER VI
Creating an Ordered World

INTRODUCTION

Trevor, a high school senior, has a good friend named Steve. For several days Steve has been urging Trevor to join with some other friends to steal street construction signs for party decorations. Trevor gets along well with his mother and usually avoids doing things which he knows will upset her. He is caught between making a decision based on the approval of Steve or on the approval of his mother.

This kind of cognitive conflict can stimulate development toward a Stage 4 perspective and requires a particular kind of formal operation. In the section on logical development we will look at aspects of logical reasoning that specifically relate to Stage 4 social perspective.

LOGICAL REASONING: FORMAL OPERATIONS RELATED TO STAGE 4 SOCIAL PERSPECTIVE

In order to understand the logical reasoning underlying the resolution of Trevor's dilemma, we need to refer back to the problem involving a triadic relationship among objects. In that problem, we found two objects, Sticks A and C, related to one another only through a third object, Stick B. Similarly, Trevor has a dyadic relationship with his friend Steve, called "A," and with his mother, called "C." In his moral dilemma, Trevor is caught between jeopardizing one of the relationships, no matter what he decides. Suddenly, after hearing for years about "laws," they make sense to him. He no longer sees law as something you obey to avoid punishment, or to gain approval; he now understands law as an abstraction which structures the chaos of living within a series of unconnected dyads. Because of this overarching system of common rules and laws to which Trevor, his friend, and his mother can all subscribe, individuals need not relate to one another personally, but may relate through this system which orders all of life and creates a structured system of triadic relationships. Trevor can appeal to the law and not have to make a choice between friend and mother. The expectation that each of them will also subscribe to this system forms in his mind a firm triadic social structure. (However, if his friend's logical reasoning and social perspective are at a lower developmental level, Trevor's decision may be viewed by Steve as a rejection of friendship or "being chicken.")

A second aspect of logical reasoning that relates specifically to Stage 4 is that of dichotomizing, described earlier. Briefly defined, it means to perceive conflicting values in terms of either/or choices—one choice is seen as correct, therefore the others must be wrong. Imagining the mind as a "mental scaffolding" as suggested in chapter 5, or a "jungle gym" set up in the head, may be helpful in understanding how thinking can move from compartmentalization which is peculiar to Stage 3 to dichotomizing which is characteristic of Stage 4 (figure 1). In

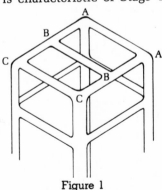

Figure 1

compartmentalization, if a thought is "moving" from C to B or is "sitting on" B, the mind is aware only of B. It can return to C only when directed by some external force or situation.

In dichotomizing, the mind is always aware of both B and C. When torn between B and C, it makes a choice, is aware of choosing, and then values the choice made. The alternative is perceived as inferior, as having been rejected for valid reasons. This aspect of logical reasoning is crucial for Stage 4 social perspective in which dichotomy is applied to value systems rather than to concrete objects and ideas (as found in concrete operations).

SOCIAL PERSPECTIVE

CONVENTIONAL LEVEL: STAGE 4

Trevor's situation of being torn between friend and mother illustrates one of the unresolved problems of Stage 3: a conflict between two sources of values. When this occurs at Stage 3, an individual has no structure which can mediate between the two. The resolution of such a conflict through a triadic structure is characteristic of Stage 4.

A woman wrote of just such a problem that confronted her when her college roommate confided that she was involved in a sexual affair with a boyfriend.

> The conflict between home and church values, and peer values, was acute and very painful. I resolved the issue for me by determining that the rules concerning premarital sex were clear—and it was up to each individual whether they kept the rules, and I had to decide for me. . . . It was a challenge to live within the law.

Notice that this woman is aware of conflicting values about right and wrong and is clearly aware of making a choice. Notice also that she does not choose between one set of relationships or the other, but instead sees a third option. This is an example of how the abstract concept of law or rule orders life, providing a common overarching structure yet differentiating the values of the self from those of others. With a Stage 4 perspective, one looks back on earlier perspectives and sees the confusion and chaos of either "doing one's own thing" or of "trying to please everybody." To avoid a return to this condition, the maintenance of rules and laws and societal structure becomes an overriding concern, and the basis for conscience and for making decisions about what is morally right. At Stage 4, relationships of affection continue to be important, but there is also an emotional investment in maintaining the social system because it is perceived that without this bridging structure conflicting values could destroy relationships. How this new structure permeates Stage 4 social perspective is seen in the description of the six factors which follow.

Concepts of Law

"Law is an absolute necessity for societal stability."

"Law is for the good of all, for the ordering of society, to make things function smoothly."

"Law is a necessary part of society living and human life would be impossible without society, like it would be impossible without some normal set-up of laws."

These are characteristic Stage 4 descriptions of law. All relationships are regulated through this third element which orders society, religion, and other institutions. The fuzziness of a Stage 3 world-view is now differentiated by well-defined boundaries at Stage 4. "We need laws, it'd be complete chaos if we didn't have them. We need clearly defined boundaries, or you run into the problem of what kind of a precedent is set, and anybody can come along and say, well, the law doesn't apply in this case."

Laws to prevent concrete destructive acts are not enough. Laws as guidelines for good behavior are not enough. Laws which can be circumvented through an individual's definition of a "good" intention are not enough. A Stage 4 concept of law provides the basic structure for a Stage 4 concept of society as a system.

Concepts of Society

A concept of society might be represented by a box. At Stage 4, laws, rules, traditions, and sanctions are the sides of the box which hold a person's world-view together (figure 2). The box may represent the person's nation, religion, or any institution of which the person feels that he or she is an integral part.

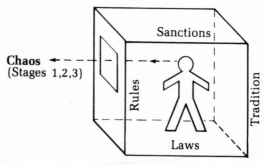

Figure 2

This world-view is constructed as if it were confirmed by laws, rules, traditions, and sanctions, and anything that threatens to break the sides of the box threatens to destroy the entire world-view or system. Looking back from within this new structure one can see the chaos which existed before the individual constructed the box, and when threatened with its possible destruction, the individual will doggedly protect this world-view just as Janie persistently defended her image of the change in the amount of clay in the clay balls!

Here, the alliance of the affective (emotional) and the cognitive is very clear. An individual's construction of the world, the box, is a cognitive structure which takes on symbolic meaning and then becomes the object of intense feelings. How strongly an individual clings to the

individual to take the role of persons committed to other values.

On the other hand, it enables a person to understand how others can also be committed to their own systems. In our research project using the Matthew 12:9-14 text (see Appendix B), one of the questions asked was: *From the standpoint of society, were the Pharisees justified in being upset with Jesus?* Only those persons who were scored primarily at Stage 4 or higher were able to put themselves in the place of the Pharisees, as exemplified in these statements:

> Well, yeah, they had to answer to their society. You've got to understand that they have their own standards, and I suppose by their standards you just flat should not break the law. If they were upset about it they would say, that, well, we have decided that any breaking of the law is bad for society.

> Yes, because he posed a very definite threat to the stability of society.

Concepts of Authority

Authority is awarded to the system itself and to those persons who are its authorized representatives. Such authority is present in elected officials, leaders of ideological movements, properly credentialed members of professions and vocational specialties. Among the academic communities, the Ph.D. is the badge of authority, a sanction by the system. However, at Stage 4, unlike Stage 3, the person is separated from the role of authority. Authority is now perceived as earned and can be withdrawn if it ceases to be deserved. So, there is movement in the direction of the self as the source of authority, as the criterion for making choices. This is clearly demonstrated in the earlier quote: ". . . it was up to each individual whether they kept the rules, and I had to decide that for me. . . . It was a challenge to live within the law." However, the basis for such authority is still determined by the system.

Value of Human Life

In the welter of laws and societal structures of Stage 4, where does the value of human life find a place? Here are some statements describing the relative worth of human and animal life:

> "A person is more important than an animal, because humans are capable of emotion and several other processes . . . humans are more complex . . . animals are not conscious, they don't think, they're not in control."

> "All life, human or otherwise, is sacred."

> "Animal life cannot be considered sacred or on a par with human life."

As at Stage 3, we find many conclusions. But at Stage 4 the value of human life is not derived, from its usefulness as at Stage 2 nor from affectional relationships as at Stage 3; rather, its basis is found in something transcendent to itself—a system or an ideology. For example, it is interesting to note that the two conflicting answers above ("All life . . . is sacred" and "Animal life cannot be considered sacred") are each justified by a reference to the sacred or religious. The underlying structure that determines value is a system, in this case "the sacred." The conclusions are content, perhaps derived from different systems or from varying interpretations of a single system.

The other response defines, the value of human life according to systems or ideologies related to scientific or humanistic values: "humans are more complex," "animals don't think."

Concepts of Persons

In the perception of persons and how they relate to one another, there is a progression from the egocentric and individualistic perspective of Stages 1 and 2 to the view from within a dyad or small group (Stage 3) to a perspective shared by a system in the larger society. At

Stage 4 the person speaks of "us or we members of society" rather than referring to society as "they," common at lower stages.

One's role as a citizen or responsible member of a system is not in terms of good intentions and helpfulness (Stage 3), but rather in terms of one's duty to contribute to society and to help maintain it. Persons who shirk such responsibilities do not deserve the rewards meted out by the system. For instance, welfare programs are often criticized on the basis that "Anyone who really wants to work can get a job, and if those people aren't willing to work, why should our tax money go to support them?" Factual information about the plight of many welfare recipients may not alter this point of view, because it is grounded in a societal ideology that hard work is always rewarded and that anybody can get ahead.

This demonstrates one of the limitations in role-taking at Stage 4. Those who do not share one's views and values may be seen as "wrong" or different, as outsiders needing conversion or persuasion to one's own point of view. This is what is meant by an exclusive society, one which excludes those who do not buy its values or subscribe to its point of view. The question is "Are you one of us?" "America: Love It Or Leave It" also may express this perspective. Persons are valued in a general way for the quality and quantity of their allegiance to systems: national, cultural, religious, or institutional.

MORAL REASONING

CONVENTIONAL LEVEL: STAGE 4
Should Heinz steal the drug for his wife? Why?

"Well, he should probably steal the drug, not probably, he should steal the drug. Very basically, because human life is sacred, is more important than law.

"Yes, I think he should steal the drug even though it's clearly against the law and even though he would put himself in jeopardy of being caught and sent to jail, sentenced. I guess my basic qualification would be that he would steal it, being aware of the consequences."

The person making these statements demonstrates some aspects of his social perspective and how they are used in the making of moral decisions. His perspective involves an understanding of human life as sacred, an awareness of the importance of the law, and an obligation to accept the consequences of breaking it. The consequences are not mitigated by "good intentions," as at Stage 3. Key concepts at Stage 4 are duty, responsibility, and obligation as defined by a system. Conscience is experienced as dishonor or institutionalized blame, not living up to societal standards. Guilt is occasioned when as the consequence of one's actions harm is done to others.

The justice structure of Stage 4 is no longer a matter of helping those who are "good" or in need of help. Rather, it involves an orientation to the third element, the society or system. Society rewards those who contribute to it and punishes those who do not. Kohlberg says that according to Stage 4 "vengeance is the right of society and is conceived not as vengeance but as 'paying your debt to society.' . . . Stage 4 justice . . . is the pattern of maintaining the distribution of reward and punishment in an already existing system . . . justice and maintenance of the basic rules and structure of society are much the same."[1]

Law, therefore, is a major concern, giving rise to the term "law and order" to describe this stage. However, this label means law only as a reflection of the complex values of a particular society, at least according to an individual's perception of them. "Right" at Stage 4 is not sticking to the letter of the law, but is primarily the maintenance of society and the protection of its welfare. Laws can justifiably be broken in the interests of preserving society itself or its primary values. At Stage 4, illegal actions in the interest of national security could be justified for such a reason, particularly when the individual sees that as his duty. Egil Krogh, who authorized the break-in of the office of Daniel Ellsberg's psychiatrist, explained his decision in such a way:

I see now that the key is the effect that the term "national security" had on my judgment. The very words served to block my critical analysis. . . . to suggest that national security was being improperly invoked was to invite a confrontation with patriotism and loyalty and so appeared to be beyond the scope and in contravention of the faithful performance of the duties of my office. . . . the very definition of national security was for the President to pursue his planned course.[2]

Taking the legal consequences of illegal actions is a part of moral decision-making at Stage 4.

Question: Should the judge sentence Heinz for stealing?

Oh, I think he should be sentenced . . . because it is his [the judge's] role to maintain and uphold the law, and his personal opinion cannot go above the law because he is not in a position as one individual to make law and to reverse law. His role is to protect societal stability. If he really felt a lot of sympathy for Heinz he could not release him anyway.

At Stage 3 the judge's sympathy for Heinz is sufficient reason for not sentencing him. At Stage 4, the orientation is to the system and its roles rather than to personal feelings and sympathies.

It is significant that authority has again become a critical issue after the relativism of Stage 2 and the emphasis on individual relationships and feelings at Stage 3. However, Stage 4 authority is located in society and its representatives rather than in powerful individuals as at Stage 1, and it is important to keep this distinction in mind.

I also want to point out again that at all stages there is concern for law and life, for punishment and authority. These are some of the basic issues which come into conflict with one another. But the understandings of these issues, and the reasons for concern, are different at each stage. Stage 4 moral reasoning is based in a complex structure of logical thinking requiring formal operations and in a complex social perspective involving the abstract idea of triadic relationships.

Back to the Heinz dilemma. *Should Heinz steal the drug?* Some reasons favoring the stealing are given at the first part of this section on moral reasoning. "Con" responses, reasoning that Heinz should not steal, are more difficult to find, but one "con" response is as follows: "I don't know if he should, he wouldn't have the compulsion. I have this thing with property rights. You can't have human rights without property rights. If you are willing to destroy someone's property, you are probably willing to destroy someone's life. But I feel quite strongly about the value of human life."[3]

In our research more respondents at Stage 4 seem to consider the conflict between the issues of human life and law resolved in favor of saving the life and accepting the legal consequences for stealing. The value of human life and responsibility for it took top priority. Some, however, found themselves in an unresolvable dilemma when they considered the role of the judge in our social system. For example,

Question: *Thinking in terms of society, what would be the best reasons for the judge to not give Heinz some sentence?*

Well, his basic responsibility is to society and to the maintenance of that society. He must also keep in mind that society is valuable as it assists the quality of human life, so if he maintains . . . well, okay, the judge could . . . I can't do it. I can't answer that question 'cause I can't put the judge out of his role as judge . . . it won't work.

It is this kind of cognitive conflict at Stage 4 which may trigger development toward Stage 5 reasoning.

Summary of Stage 4

Stage 4 is an advance over Stage 3 in that it embodies a complex social system which provides limits and guidelines for responsible decision-making. But it has great difficulty resolving conflicts between life and law and between civil rights and law where its tendency to dichotomize limits concern for individual universal rights.

Yet in a society such as ours which is permeated with relativism, the well-defined boundaries of a Stage 4 system tend to become blurred. Persons ready to move from the inadequacies of a Stage 3 perspective may find few systems in our society with clearly defined limits. Here is a poignant excerpt from a letter by a high school student to his parents in which he expresses frustration at the lack of such a model.

Then all the Watergate stuff—is there anybody to believe in, to trust? I need to hear you say what's good about our government instead of complaining about taxes and who is a crook. Does our system really work? I hear so many gripes, I'm very discouraged and wonder if it's worth growing up, going to college, or getting a job.[4]

Another young man claims, "The principal is just waiting for me to break another rule so he can throw me out of school." He perceives authority and rules in a very personal way, with both being used against him. What he needs to hear at this point in his development is the positive value of rules, that rules and structure prevent the principal from "throwing him out" according to personal whim.

In a relativistic society, how far can relativism be carried before the society itself collapses because laws, traditions, and standards are turned to amorphous jelly? How can the structures that hold society together be presented so that they stimulate development toward a Stage 4 perspective without becoming legalistic ends in themselves? Taking a serious look at developmental theory raises such questions, and they will be dealt with further in subsequent chapters.

At Stage 4, the concrete symbol becomes separated from the meaning behind it. The meaning is now understood in terms of abstract ideas, although these ideas tend to be oversimplified. The flag may represent country, patriotism, democracy, or other images, but this concrete object is not the same thing as any of these ideas. The Bible may represent a variety of religious concepts, but it is understood that those concepts can exist without the book. At times the symbol may be perceived as a negation of meaning, or as unrelated to its original meaning. In such instances, the symbol loses its power to evoke meaning. The functioning of symbols is a challenge to the parent and other educators charged with the transmission of cultural or religious values.

SUMMARY OF THE CONVENTIONAL LEVEL

There has been a progression in social perspective from the **Preconventional Level** in which the SELF is the center, to the **Conventional Level** in which persons take their social understandings from their familiar social and cultural milieu. In the latter perspective, the center becomes the COMMUNITY/SOCIETY. There are a greater number of choices available and increasing freedom to choose as persons travel the road from egocentrism to ever-enlarging circles of reference.

It is estimated that at least two-thirds of the adults in the United States share the conventional world-view and for whom it is reality. Reality is wherever one is on the developmental journey; a structure (stage) filled in with information of a specific content. It is exceedingly difficult to accept a reality different from one's own because each of us feels that what one knows is real. The specific content of a structure may be national understandings, religious beliefs, and/or political views. Whatever the content, Stage 4 tends to take an either/or stand, a dichotomizing position, in relation to content.

Stage 3 may be found as early as eight years of age and becomes common during later adolescence. Stage 4 may appear in the late teens.

In the next chapter we will take a look at what happens to cognitive structure when conventional perspectives no longer suffice as the basis for understanding the self, the world, and right and wrong.

QUIZ

TRUE/FALSE

T/F

1. Two characteristics of logical reasoning underlying Stage 4 are triadic structure and dichotomizing. ____
2. Triadic structure can resolve conflicts created by Stage 3 perspective. ____
3. In compartmentalization, the mind moves more freely on the "mental scaffolding" than in dichotomizing. ____
4. At Stage 4, a major concern is the maintenance of the system of rules, laws, and social structures. ____
5. There may be a strong cognitive basis for an emotional response. ____
6. A system defines the values for those committed to it. ____
7. At any stage, persons can take the role of others in relation to their commitments to systems. ____
8. At Stage 4 there is movement in the direction of seeing the self as the authority. ____
9. At Stage 4, justice and maintenance of the basic rules and structure of society are much the same. ____
10. The developmental journey is one of increasing differentiation and integration, with more available choices and increasing freedom to choose. ____

ANSWERS
1. T 2. T 3. F 4. T 5. T 6. T 7. F 8. T 9. T
10. T

AN EXERCISE

You are a teacher or leader of a class or group of high school seniors. The youth are complaining about the arbitrary nature of school rules, and about the unfairness of school and civil authorities and regulations. You suspect that cheating, truancy, and drug and alcohol use are common forms of behavior among these young persons.

1. List some Stage 2 and 3 reasons which you think the youth might give to justify their rule-breaking behavior.

2. List some reasons from Stages 2, 3, and 4 which might support rule-obeying behavior. (This may stimulate movement toward Stage 4 reasoning.)

3. How convincing do you think these last reasons might be to the members of the class or group?

4. Describe some activities for your class or group which might stimulate a Stage 4 social perspective and moral reasoning.

SOME POSSIBLE ANSWERS

1. At Stage 2, you remember, laws and rules serve to prevent concrete destructive acts. If there are no visible results from behavior, rules do not apply. If they are enforced, they may be seen as ways in which authorities "try to be the big cheese," as one adolescent put it. An individual's behavior is "not the problem" of authorities; they should "mind their own business." Cheating may be fair if other people are doing it, in order to protect one's own interests.

   At Stage 3, the behavior and approval of one's peers or parental example may sanction rule- and law-breaking: "Everybody else does it." "My dad always speeds; he breaks laws." "My parents cheat on their income tax."

2. The approval of teachers and leaders who are liked may be very important to adolescents. So the following

reasons might appeal to a Stage 3 social perspective: "If you carry pot when you are in my car, and I get stopped, you could cause me tremendous trouble and embarrassment." "You could get the whole group in trouble." "I care about what happens to you."

3. Until youth have experienced the positive function of rules, laws, and society at Stages 2 and 3, they may interpret all rules as unfair power plays by authorities—a Stage 1 perspective. Therefore, Stage 4 reasons in support of rule-obeying behavior such as, "It is against the law, and law is important for order in our society" tend to be rejected.

4. Planning group activities offers rich opportunities for youth to experience the function of rules and ordered structure. Many adults tend to tell youth what the rules are. Whenever possible, youth can be helped to think through possible problems that might arise in future activities and to suggest the kinds of structures that might prevent such problems. The adult leaders need to suggest possibilities not proposed by the youth and should bring institutional concerns and regulations to their attention. Here we are talking about participation in the democratic process of decision-making, further described as "the just community" in chapter 9.

CHAPTER VII
Out of the Box: Beyond Convention

INTRODUCTION

What happens when the limits of a Stage 4 perspective are reached—when the enclosing structure of the conventional world-view is shaken by visions of a more open world beyond—when the sides of the box seem to constrict rather than support?

In this chapter we will look first at some characteristics of logical reasoning, which involve more complex formal operations, enabling a person to construct a different world-view. Secondly, we will briefly explore different paths which individuals appear to take as they face limitations in their conventional structures. And finally we will look at descriptions of Stage 5 social perspective and moral reasoning. Because of the complexity and rarity of the postconventional structure, descriptions and distinctions among its forms are neither as clear nor as well understood as they are at other levels.

LOGICAL REASONING:
MORE COMPLEX FORMAL OPERATIONS

The mental operations in dialectical thinking and synthesizing underlie the postconventional structure. Synthesizing, the more complex foundation, is especially evident at the highest stages of social perspective and moral reasoning. Referring to the drawing of the "jungle gym" in chapter 6, we perceive that the mind is now able to move freely back and forth between B, C, and A. This is dialectical thinking.[1] Alternatives are always available and can be sampled at will. The best of each can then be appropriated and weighed against other options. The mind lives with ambiguity and paradox, seeking always to reconcile contradictions and to resolve conflicts.

The ultimate step the mind takes in moving all over the jungle gym is to step outside it and take it as a whole—to see the synthesis of all its elements. This formal operation of synthesis is the basis for the most complex structures of social perspective and moral reasoning, and is also what Fowler relates to Stage 6 faith development.[2]

TRANSITIONS IN SOCIAL
PERSPECTIVE AND MORAL REASONING

When Stage 4 perspective is shaken or ceases to function in adequate ways, the threat may be more than an individual is able to tolerate, which may cause the rejection of new possibilities. "I know what my values are, and I just don't want to even think about any new ideas." In such a case, the person may become fixed at Stage 4, at least temporarily and perhaps permanently.

A second transitional response is the complete rejection of the old structure and/or content, an attempt to shed it as a snake sheds its skin.

I've been taught all my life that a human life is more important than animal life, but when you get right down to thinking about it, I don't believe any of the reasons like God made man to be above the beasts. Also, the law says so, and I have to live within the law.
Why Do You Have to Live Within the Law?
To make my life more comfortable, a very selfish reason.

The young woman quoted here gives an example of the relativism that is found in some persons moving out of Stage 4. When Kohlberg and his researchers first identified this structure, it was thought to be a regression to Stage 2 because of the relativistic and apparently egocentric orientation.[3] It is now understood as the rejection of a Stage 4 perspective by persons moving outside it, and is called Stage 4½. At the time of this interview, the young woman just quoted described the

137

way she felt because of her confusion about values as "being caught in an elevator between floors." She had rejected many of her previous standards, or at least the reasons for them, but was unable to find new ones to take their place.

Unable to live comfortably between floors, yet finding it impossible to return to the social perspective from which they have come, some of these transitional persons construct new social systems or ideologies, which are different in content, but similar in structure, to the ones they have rejected.[4] These new systems may take many forms: social activist groups, radically different religious groups, or militant organizations. (However, participation in such groups is not necessarily an indication of Stage 4½. Persons may find such activities attractive for a variety of reasons unrelated to specific stages. Although stages can to some extent predict behavior, behavior can never indicate stage!)

Others may turn to hedonism or even illegal activities, finding justification in their perspective of complete relativism. Some may search for community in the small group movement where closeness, openness, and "being in touch" are valued in an attempt to fill the void left by their "non-society" perspective.[5] The emphasis is on the self. (The so-called "value-free" approach of values clarification is consistent with a Stage 4½ world-view. But again, it must be reiterated that this does not mean that any person who participates in small groups or values clarification strategies is doing so for Stage 4½ reasons. Such activities are valuable for different reasons at different stages, and for reasons that have nothing to do with stages.) At Stage 4½, individuals may also reject concepts of historical time and tradition, excluding the past from their world-view and choosing experiences based in the here and now. (Again, we cannot reverse the theory and infer Stage 4½ whenever we observe this attitude.)

I do not have sufficient data to describe adequately the

six factors of social perspective for Stage 4½. Stage 4½ moral reasoning is identified through a combination of reasons from Stages 2 through 5, with a strong element of relativism. If Heinz's wife was that important to him, he should steal the drug simply because his wife needed it.

The same person who responds thus, in a manner that can be scored as Stage 2, may describe the judge's role in conventional terms: "He's in society, it's his job to make society function. He's supposed to uphold the law, and the law would say that Heinz should be sentenced for stealing."

And the young woman who was "caught between floors" stated the value of the life of Heinz's wife in this way.

I can see where if this woman was a great scientist or someone else who was really contributing to other people's well-being, her life would be worth more, but I really don't think that's true. She has a right to have her life, no matter who she is. Any person . . . but then we come into the idea, what if she was a person who would harm other people or kill them . . . that is a problem . . . she shouldn't be allowed to do so. Now, I'm not saying she should be allowed to die just because she would do that. Anyone has as much right to live as anyone else.

In her interview, this person demonstrated Stage 2 relativism, a rejection of the conventional perspective which she gave evidence of understanding very well, and a groping toward universal principles characteristic of the postconventional perspective. In the quotation above, note that she is aware of inconsistencies and tensions; her statement is an excellent example of the person experiencing the inadequacy of his or her moral reasoning and searching for something more adequate.

A third option in the transition beyond a conventional perspective is a more direct route into Stage 5 perspective. This may involve:

1. The replacement of a static, frozen concept of society by one that is a living, growing, changing community held together by commitments and contracts

which are shared and have been agreed upon by the community,

2. an understanding of individuals as having value apart from societal definitions and roles and apart from personal sentiments,

3. a recognition of one's value as a separate individual, which allows the investment of self in the rights of others.[6]

The person at Stage 4½ has taken a detour between a conventional and postconventional perspective, a transition which may be made more directly by others. The young woman I have quoted in this chapter seems to be integrating in terms of the second and third principles above, but still may be floundering in relationship to the first one. Probably most persons move from Stage 4 to 5 without experiencing Stage 4½. But for adults, transition from any stage to another appears to be a process involving deep and challenging experiences. This is especially true for development beyond Stage 4.

SOCIAL PERSPECTIVE

A postconventional social perspective implies that the person takes a position outside of society, and thus is aware of values and rights that underlie or are prior to societal connections. Concrete laws are seen apart from the values and rights that generate them. The complex structure of logical reasoning allows the mind to roam freely over the jungle gym, perceiving, comparing, and evaluating many possibilities.

POSTCONVENTIONAL LEVEL: STAGE 5

Concepts of Law
What is the purpose and function of the law?

"Law is for the protection of universal human rights. It should—but often can't—be able to mediate between different human rights, to sort things out according to

140

priorities. If law is applied literally to every situation, it can become unreasonable as far as its intent, the purpose behind any particular law."

This person is clearly aware of the conflicting issues in the Heinz dilemma, which would also be true at Stage 4, but sees the law as trying to "mediate" rather than dichotomize, and recognizes its limitations.

A Stage 5 view of law is very complex and encompasses some or all of the ideas summarized below.

1. Laws are products of a process of decision-making by rational men and women who have contracted with one another to abide by these laws. This is called "social contract." Laws are the result of common agreement and mutual understandings, not the authoritative demands of a "big brother" society.

2. Law is a means for regulating society, including the civic and political order, but it in turn stands under the judgment of a higher order. In the United States this higher order is the judicial system which functions to ensure that laws remain consistent with individual rights and with the welfare of the majority, the greatest good for the greatest number.

3. Law protects equality of individual rights to life, liberty, and property. There is a clear perception of a hierarchy of rights, with the universal right to life seen as prior to laws and other rights. Note that this is not a hierarchy of things—life over property, for instance, but of rights.

Concepts of Society

Stage 5 moves toward understanding the principles that underlie the structure of a social system with a sense of ultimate values organized in a hierarchy.

There is a high degree of relativistic orientation because at Stage 5 one perceives that many differing social systems and religious traditions can serve humanity in appropriate ways. However, this is not the more simplistic concept of multiplicity—"One person's way is just as good as another's"—which appears at lower stages. It is rather an openness to looking at truth in ways other than one's own and is an example of dialectical thinking.

The concept of society is an open and inclusive one in which all persons have equal rights regardless of affectional ties, national or racial origin, or performance of "right roles." It is a recognition of society as it exists, from an objective point of view. It also envisions how society might become more adequate, based on fundamental values: (1) protection of civil rights, (2) social contract, (3) the greatest good for the greatest number, and (4) rational decision-making and majority vote, or due process.

Concepts of Authority

The locus of authority is now within the individual. Traditional sources of authority—other persons, groups, customs, law, tradition, and society—are taken seriously but are weighed, compared, and evaluated in a thoughtful dialectical process in which rationality is accentuated. Laws seen as mutually agreed upon social contracts may function as societal authority. But a hierarchy of values may develop concurrently with an intuition that there are principles or decisions of conscience which are above the law. However, there may be difficulty in defining these as rational moral principles. Instead, an individual may express decisions of conscience in terms of universally valid rules, values, or sentiments.

The emphasis upon rationality does not mean that persons at Stage 5 are cold and unemotional. It does mean that such persons are able to distinguish clearly between thinking and feeling, and are not satisfied with decisions based on feelings alone. At Stage 3, one's affiliation or feeling for others is paramount, but at Stage 5, it is one of many factors which must be considered and weighed.

At Stage 4, diverse and conflicting ideas are handled by either/or decisions; at Stage 5, the reality of such polarities is accepted, and one of the characteristics of a

Stage 5 perspective is the ability to recognize and accept contradiction and paradox and the resulting tensions. It may be uncomfortable, but conflicts are perceived as necessary if one is to take seriously the complexity of the world as one sees it unfolding.

Value of Human Life

Human life is more important than animal life. As far as we know, humans are the only kind of creatures who find and attribute meaning to all the rest of the universe, who can make what we call moral decisions, take ethical responsibility.

Note here the abstract concepts and the description of human life in terms of moral decision-making. Using the qualifier, "as far as we know," is an expression of the Stage 5 openness to the existence of new truths side by side with a commitment to truth as presently understood.

The value of human life at Stage 5 finds expression in terms of a generalized right to live, which takes precedence over all other rights, and in the right of individuals to make moral decisions concerning their own life or death. This is not, however, a "do your own thing" understanding, but is based in the complex of individual rights, duties, and responsibilities inherent in a Stage 5 perspective.

Concepts of Persons

All persons are seen as having equal rights regardless of their origins or roles in society. In response to the Heinz dilemma one person said:

Yes, Heinz should steal the drug . . . Because his wife's life, his wife's right to life, takes precedence over the druggist's right to property. I think it's an inherent right that every human has, the right not to be deprived of one's life by something or somebody else. It's a universal human right.

This person accorded the same right to a stranger:

It's the same thing in principle, that stranger has as much right to be saved as the wife or anybody else.

Such an overriding affirmation of the equality of rights of all humans represents the more equilibriated reasoning of Stage 5. But when individual rights come into conflict, the individual may be sacrificed as a means to achieve the greatest good for the greatest number. Where no such choices need be made, the equal rights of all are respected.

Role-Taking Ability

James W. Fowler has described Stage 5 role-taking in faith development thus: "The person has the ability not only to take the role of another person or group but also to take the role of another person's or group's world-view in its full complexity."[7]

There is a painful awareness of the differences among all individuals and groups with the knowledge that one can never know another person completely, that "truths" are never appropriated with exactly the same understandings. There is the ability to step outside of one's own point of view in order to step inside that of another. There is continuing concern for "understanding what the other person means," so that significant communication can take place in a shared search for meaning and truth.

At Stage 3 the interpretation of the Golden Rule involves putting oneself in another's shoes in regard to personal feelings. At Stage 5, role-taking involves reversibility not only of feelings, but of reciprocal rights. One looks at situations in terms of the basic and universal rights of each individual and sees an obligation to respond to those rights.

MORAL REASONING

POSTCONVENTIONAL LEVEL: STAGE 5

Moral reasoning at Stage 5 grows from the bedrock of Stage 5 social perspective and is based in a commitment to social contract, utility (the greatest good for the greatest number), and individual rights. At Stage 5 a clear distinction is made between those values which *should* be the basis for all societies, and the varieties of values which actually characterize differing societies.

There is an awareness of a hierarchy of basic rights. In answer to the question, *Should Heinz steal the drug?* we hear these responses:

Yes, life takes priority over law, and I think human rights, life, is a lot more basic than property rights.

Yes. Law protects property rights, but it also protects other human rights including the right to life which takes precedence over the right to property. Where the two rights come into conflict as in this case, I would say that Heinz is completely justified in stealing the drug on a moral basis, and he might also win his case on a legal basis.

These statements demonstrate an integration and differentiation of conflicting issues. Contradictions left unresolved at the **Conventional Level** are now analyzed dialectically and synthetically. A Stage 5 societal perspective is seen in the following response to the question, *Can you think of some reasons why people who break the law should be punished?*

Well, you have to look at the intent of the law and if the intent of the law is to provide a way in which people can live together in harmony, in which people can live with one another's rights being naturalized, somebody who violates that then violates in a sense the rights of all the rest.

What is ultimately right is that which supports the good of all and the rights of individuals.

As already suggested by the quotations, the *process* of decision-making takes precedence over set or fixed bodies of rule or law. Essential to this process—known as due process—is the representation of all interested individuals or groups in such a way that minority views and individual liberties are recognized. Underlying this orientation is the concept of a social contract, in which participants freely agree to its terms. Once such an agreement has been reached, the contract itself assumes

145

the position of authority. But basic to it is the initial decision of persons to enter into a contractual relationship.

At Stage 5, moral reasoning tends to emphasize consistency and rationality in the decision-making process and is able to construct and analyze alternate points of view. It should not be concluded, however, that this is a totally cold and impersonal process. Rather, it is characterized by the ability to distinguish the varieties of factors which may enter into the decision-making process, and to know the difference between emotional and rational decisions. The decisions of Stage 5 may well emerge from intense emotional struggles with systems that perpetuate injustice and indignity. Such a passionate commitment to justice, understood at Stage 5 as equality of rights and the opportunity to attain other forms of equality, is basic to the civil rights movement of recent years (although there must be many distortions of these basic values).

Stage 5 is a relatively rare mode of reasoning, with estimates of its frequency of occurrence in the United States ranging from 5 to 10 percent of the adult population. It is seldom found in persons younger than their late twenties in age.

In answer to the question, *Should Heinz steal the drug?* pro answers are the rule, and con answers are seldom encountered. Previously in this section I have given several examples of pro responses. In my research, I have found no answers at Stage 5 in support of not stealing the drug. Nevertheless, Stage 5 seems consistently to affirm obeying the law.

Should people do everything they can to obey the law?

Yes. Why? Well, because I think the purpose of the law is to ensure that people's rights are protected and . . . so . . . basically it needs to be obeyed unless these rights appear to be denied by the way the law is carried out. You see, laws are a very concrete kind of way of being sure that people's rights are protected.

146

SUMMARY OF STAGE 5

Kohlberg calls the Stage 5 orientation to society the "prior-to-society perspective." He describes it as the

perspective of a rational individual aware of values and rights prior to social attachments and contracts. Integrates perspectives by formal mechanisms of agreement, contract, objective impartiality, and due process. Considers moral and legal points of view; recognizes that they sometimes conflict and finds it difficult to integrate them.[8]

There is an awareness of the relativity of many values, and there is ability to distinguish between those values that are part of one's group or society and those that are universal.

The consistent use of a Stage 5 perspective in moral decision-making is rare, and may well be forged from personal experiences of conflict with Stage 4 institutional structures. Such a possibility is suggested by Dan Candee's research into the Watergate affair.

The progression to Stage 4 is marked by the awareness that individual relationships are part of a larger society. Roles become structured with definite duties and privileges. The overriding concern in Stage 4 is to maintain a system which allows the society to function smoothly and avoids chaos. Such a system need not be conventional society; it may be an "ideal" system, humanistic, religious, or communal. But if the system itself is seen as more basic than the rights of its individual members, it is being viewed from a Stage 4 perspective.

A classic instance of such reasoning seems to have motivated former chief plumber, Egil Krogh, to have authorized the break-in at the office of Dr. Fielding, Daniel Ellsberg's psychiatrist. Recalling his reasoning at the time, Krogh reflects:

"I see now that the key is the effect that the term 'national security' had on my judgment. The very words served to block my critical analysis . . . to suggest that national security was being improperly invoked was to invite a confrontation with patriotism and loyalty and so appeared to be beyond the scope and in contravention of the faithful performance of the duties of

147

my office. . . . the very definition of national security was for the President to pursue his planned course."

As Krogh saw it, his primary duty was fulfill the requirements of his role, not to insure human rights.[9]

Candee says that he was unable to find any Stage 5 reasoning among the Watergate participants, but he does quote a statement by former Special Prosecutor Archibald Cox as an example of such reasoning.[10]

If man is by nature a social being—if we are destined to live and work together—if our goal is the freedom of each to choose the best he can discern—if we seek to do what we can to move toward the realization of these beliefs, then the rights of speech, privacy, dignity and other fundamental liberties of other men such as the Bill of Rights declares, must be respected by both government and private persons.

Candee then goes on to say that the Watergate experience appears to have been a catalyst for moral growth on the part of Egil Krogh. He writes:

Compare Krogh's earlier statement [above] with his reflections upon being sentenced for directing the break-in at the office of Daniel Ellsberg's psychiatrist:
"But however national security is defined, I now see that none of the potential uses of the sought information could justify the invasion of the rights of the individuals that the break-in necessitated. The understanding I have come to is that *these rights are the definition of our nation.* . . ."[11] *(italics added)*

Perhaps the reader has recognized in the quotation above one of the statements which opened chapter 1. The three opening quotations exemplify an abbreviated developmental journey: Stage 1, Stage 3, and Stage 5. Krogh's statements demonstrate to some extent the kind of struggle that may stimulate Stage 5 reasoning, although for most persons the struggle probably would not involve such dramatic conflict with the legal system.

According to Fowler, Stage 5 function of symbols rejoins the emotional and the aesthetic with the *idea* and sees the partiality of the symbol in his or her system of meaning.[12] This may mean that the symbol itself simply points to a reality beyond it, but the relationships between the reality and the symbol are synthesized into a meaningful experience. For instance, it is recognized that the flag is not itself the reality of the nation, or of patriotic sentiments, but that it does invoke and express both one's ideas and one's feelings about the nation. In the same way, the Bible carries the commitments of a religious tradition and evokes strong feelings about it, but it is not the same thing as the faith toward which it points, and which it represents.

Stage 5 is the most complex stage for which we have data derived from interviews. In the next chapter we look at a more elusive construct of meaning, Stage 6, or what I call "the shaping vision."

QUIZ

Match the statements in Column A with their completions in Column B.

Column A	Column B
1. The mental operations which underlie postconventional structure are _____	1. social contract, utility, and individual rights.
2. When a Stage 4 perspective is shaken, a person may _____	2. all persons have equal rights.
3. A postconventional social perspective implies that a person takes a position _____	3. dialectical thinking and synthesizing.
4. At Stage 5 the concept of society is an open and inclusive one in which _____	4. outside of or prior to society.
5. At Stage 5 traditional sources of authority are taken seriously but are _____	5. reject new ideas, reject their Stage 4 world-view, adopt a new ideology, start to develop Stage 5 thinking.
6. Moral reasoning at Stage 5 is based in a commitment to _____	6. weighed, compared, and evaluated.

ANSWERS

1. 3   2. 5   3. 4   4. 2   5. 6   6. 1

AN EXERCISE

Here is a good exercise to help you review all the stages and imagine how they might function in a real-life situation. The exercise is most effective when it is role-played by a group of persons who have been studying this material. However, individuals can also work out ways to role-play each stage.

DIRECTIONS

Describe a decision-making situation that is relevant to the participants. Here are some possibilities:

1. A task force of citizens, teachers, and school board members trying to decide whether or not the school district should eliminate values and humanistic education and get back to the basics.
2. A similar task force trying to decide whether or not to introduce sex education programs into the school system.
3. A task force of parents, church school teachers, and church education committee members trying to decide on a new curriculum for the church school in a situation where a number of people have been complaining that there is not enough Bible study in the curriculum.
4. A meeting of a city council and citizens concerning whether or not a large area of land should be sold to developers for apartments or bought by the city for park and recreation facilities.

Using possibility 1 (above), describe the various roles to be played in the following way:
  citizen at Stage 1
  teacher at Stage 1
  school board member at Stage 2
  teacher at Stage 2
  citizen at Stage 3

151

school board member at Stage 3 (chairperson of the meeting)
teacher at Stage 4
school board member at Stage 4
citizen at Stage 5
teacher at Stage 5

Divide the total group into five smaller groups, assigning a different stage to each group. Each group will then discuss how persons at the assigned stage might understand the issues and reason about them. They may want to look at such factors as locus of authority, role-taking, and function of symbols. Two persons will be chosen by each group to represent the two roles assigned for that stage.

Chairs are arranged for the task force meeting so that the rest of the group can observe. Role-players take their places and the meeting is opened by the assigned chairperson. Role-players attempt to reason in the meeting according to their assigned stage.

Continue the meeting until ideas begin to be repetitive or are slow in coming. At that time, call it to a close and begin sharing reflections.

First, role-players are encouraged to share what they were feeling during the meeting and what they were thinking about those feelings. Then the other group members can make observations and try to guess who represented which stage. A major discussion question is: What effect did reasoning at different stages have on group process? It is ordinarily very apparent that the existence of different stages within a group is a major source of communication difficulties.

A GUIDED FANTASY

Another way of reviewing the stages, which I have used with classes, is the following guided fantasy. If you use this with a group, first give a brief overview of procedures. Tell the group that no one needs to participate who does not want to and that anyone may stop participating at any point. Then read slowly, allowing time for imaginations to work. Before you start, ask each person to have paper and pencil handy.

"You may want to close your eyes . . . Imagine yourself waking up, standing in a completely strange town in a completely strange setting. You are on a winding street. You can see other streets leading from it at different angles, some straight, some winding . . . without pattern. There are no street signs . . . no street numbers . . . no directional signs . . . You wander on different streets, intrigued by new sights, not caring where you have been or where you are going.

But then you become confused, and a purple or an orange balloon appears overhead, and the person in the balloon tells you what to do and where to go. You sleep or eat someplace, but when you leave you don't know where you have been unless you happen to come upon that place again. Everything flows together and much of life is made up of pleasant surprises because of the unexpected and magical kinds of things that happen.

"Now open your eyes . . . Using your paper and pencil, draw a picture of this town."

After allowing time for people to complete their pictures, suggest that they again close their eyes.

"You have learned your way around the town. You know the landmarks, you know when to turn, which way to go. You can move easily from one familiar place to another. You have learned that the people in the balloons appear in certain places, at certain times. As long as you keep your eye on the familiar landmarks, buildings, trees, houses, you can't get lost. Many things are predictable, and follow an orderly and logical sequence.

"Now open your eyes and draw a picture of this town
. . .

153

"Close your eyes again if you wish . . . You have lived in the town a long time. You no longer consciously look for landmarks. The streets are familiar and comfortable and you have a picture or map of them in your mind. The people in the balloons have friendly familiar faces and can be trusted to take care of emergencies because they are good people. Sometimes someone says, 'Aren't the streets confusing, why don't you put up street signs?' But, you say, 'That's the way the town is, everyone knows that, and if it's not clear we don't need to worry because the balloon people will help.'

"Now open your eyes and draw a picture of this town
. . .

"Close your eyes . . . You've learned a lot more about the town. You now know that the streets were built to conform to the houses. You can see the complexity of the whole system. When someone suggests straightening some of the streets, you know that that would destroy the pattern of the town. You see the important role of the balloon people in keeping the system in working order. You think that street signs would help to ensure a more orderly functioning of the system.

"Now open your eyes and draw a picture of this town
. . .

"Close your eyes and imagine that you are taking your first ride in a purple balloon. You are floating above your town, and you can see other nearby towns. You see good and bad things about all the towns, you compare them, and you get new ideas for changing and improving the system of your town. But when you return to earth and try to explain to other people who haven't been up in the balloon, they can't imagine what things look like from up there. You describe how insignificant some things look, but the people who haven't been up there can only see these things as big and important. You wish everyone could go up in the balloon.''

This is a fantasy trip through the stages. Give the group an opportunity to reflect on their feelings and pictures and to share with other members if they wish.

CHAPTER VIII
The Shaping Vision

INTRODUCTION

What Kohlberg orginally described as Stage 6 of moral reasoning is so infrequently—if ever—encountered in interviews that a definitive description is not clear. There is little concensus at present about the validity of Kohlberg's Stage 6 as a basis for moral reasoning, or about its relationship to Stage 5. Stage 6 may be seen as a philosophical construction of an ideal world-view. I perceive it as "the shaping vision," a vision of justice, mercy, and love in which persons are seen as ends, not means. This vision is elusive, it may change in form, beckoning us to fuller understandings, and it *may* shape the content of all the other stages. I want to stress that my presentation of Stage 6 is more impressionistic and less complete than that of other stages.

LOGICAL REASONING

Underlying this highest stage is the logical operation of synthesizing, the combining of diverse ideas into a coherent whole, as already described in chapter 7.

SOCIAL PERSPECTIVE

POSTCONVENTIONAL LEVEL: STAGE 6

Kohlberg briefly describes the social perspective of Stage 6 as follows:

Perspective of a moral point of view from which social arrangements derive. Perspective is that of any rational individual recognizing the nature of morality or the fact that persons are ends in themselves and must be treated as such.[1]

He calls this the stage of universal ethical principles. It's rarity is reflected in the fact that the current *Scoring Guide* does not include Stage 6.[2]

Concepts of Society

Society is understood in terms of a universal morality beyond social contract and equal rights. A Stage 6 concept of community/society can only be suggested at this point. Robert G. Kegan describes it thus:

When the individual finds himself standing in the history of that [Stage 5] compact or contract, *as well as* his own personal history, he finds himself living at the still burning end of the comet that is that contract, just as much as he lives on the leading edge of his own life.[3]

This may mean a reappropriation of one's tradition—religious and/or secular; the ability to live with the past as it meets with the present, at the growing edge of the fusion of past and present and of individual and community, seen as an equilibrated (balanced and integrated) whole in the lives of single individuals. In the societal context of a constitutional community such as the United States of America, this idea might be represented diagrammatically as in Figure 1 below; a religious context could also be superimposed or substituted. In this world-view we can see an excellent example of the synthesizing function of the mind!

Concepts of Persons and the Value of Human Life

Stage 6 goes beyond the concept of equal rights and considers each individual as an end, not as the means to any other end, even when that end might be the welfare of all or the greatest good for the greatest number. This might be called "respect for personality," the giving of equal consideration to the claims of all persons—a commitment to the unconditional value of persons.

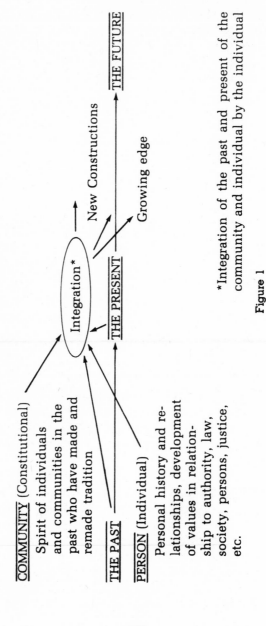

COMMUNITY (Constitutional)
Spirit of individuals and communities in the past who have made and remade tradition

THE PAST

PERSON (Individual)
Personal history and relationships, development of values in relationship to authority, law, society, persons, justice, etc.

Integration*

THE PRESENT

New Constructions

Growing edge

THE FUTURE

*Integration of the past and present of the community and individual by the individual

Figure 1

Concepts of Law

Law is understood in much the same way as at Stage 5, but in addition serves to ensure that equal consideration is given to the claims of all persons above and beyond the protection of certain rights and the welfare of the majority. At this stage, the right to life of Heinz's wife defines a *correlative* duty to act in her behalf, and in any case in which the law does not support this right, it becomes clearly subservient to individual duty.

Concepts of Authority

The paradoxical nature of authority which characterized Stage 5 is resolved at Stage 6 by integration or synthesis in which contradictions are affirmed and dealt with creatively. Locus of authority has shifted to the self in response to integrating universal moral principles.

Role-Taking Ability

In his model of faith development, Fowler describes Stage 6 role-taking in this way: "Stage Six has the ability to respond to and feel commonality with the concreteness and individuality of persons while also relating to and evoking their potential."[4]

Personhood is not confused with affection or role or value to society. Each individual is seen as an ultimate end, a center, and at the same time as fused with community. There is the capacity to take the role of a universal community, such as described in the section on concepts of community/society. This role-taking at Stage 6 takes the individual beyond the realm of idealistic words into the struggles of actual experiences.

Kohlberg uses the term "ideal role-taking" to identify the ability to take the role simultaneously of all the participants in a situation of moral choice, and in such a way that each person is treated as an end. This is not an exercise in sentimentality, but is highly complex cognitive functioning involving operations upon operations. And yet this cognitive basis in no way minimizes the possibility of intense affective involvement.

MORAL REASONING

POSTCONVENTIONAL LEVEL: STAGE 6

At Stage 6 moral reasoning is based on a commitment to ethical principles of justice that are universal, consistent, and applicable to all humankind. Kohlberg suggests two such universal principles:

1. Persons are of unconditional value which means to "act so as to treat each person as an end, not as means."

2. Individual justice, meaning "the right of every person to an equal consideration of his claims in every situation, not just those [situations] codified into law."[5]

A simplified example of such justice is the kind of fairness involved when one person cuts two pieces of pie and the other person gets to choose first. In a conflict situation, a just resolution is *one that can be agreed upon as fair by everyone involved in the situation.* This is one of the processes involved in making a moral judgment at Stage 6. Another distinctive process is that of role-taking, "taking the point of view of others conceived as *subjects* and coordinating those points of view."[6] When a reversible moral decision is reached, the process has been called "ideal role-taking." "Stage 6 moral judgment is based on role-taking, the claim of each actor under the assumption that all other actors' claims are also governed by the Golden Rule and accommodated accordingly."[7] Another way of saying this is to state that one is "under a veil of ignorance as to who in a moral situation one is to be."[8] Kohlberg goes on to explain:

Returning to the stealing-the-drug situation, let us imagine someone making the decision under the veil of ignorance, i.e., not knowing whether he is to be assigned the role of husband, wife, or druggist. Clearly, the rational solution is to steal the drug; i.e., this leads to the least loss (or the most gain) to an individual who could be in any role. This corresponds to our intuition of the primacy of the woman's right to life over the druggist's right to property and makes it a duty to act in terms of those rights. If the situation is that the dying person is a friend or acquaintance, the same holds true. Here a solution achieved under the veil of ignorance is equivalent to one obtained by ideal role-taking, or "moral musical chairs."[9]

What actually happens in such moral decision-making is that the person who is least advantaged in the situation has the same chance as everyone else. The process ensures that anyone could be in the position of Heinz's wife and would still be assured that he or she was treated as an end, and not as a means serving some other end such as the protection of property rights or the maintenance of social order. The solution is called reversible because the same perspective is taken for anyone in the situation. This perspective involves being able to look at all persons' claims impartially and to put the self in the shoes of any other (ideal role-taking).

SUMMARY OF STAGE 6

Allowing Stage 6 to function as a shaping vision rather than as a philosophical concept may accomplish several things:

—it removes Stage 6 from the realm of precise definition without cutting off discussion of its validity and its meaning,

—it allows us to participate in the ambiguity of our understanding rather than to reject Stage 6 as a theory because it doesn't meet our requirements of definition,

—it can draw us toward new understandings, stimulating our hopes and questioning our present constructions of reality.

For example, Stage 6 may symbolically represent the vision of justice that inspired the writers of the Constitution of the United States of America. Written as a Stage 5 conception of justice molded around the concept of equal rights, this vision was embodied in that document. The principles of human rights in the Constitution have been given concrete form in the laws of our nation, but the original vision of "persons as ends, not means" may go through various transformations. At Stage

4, laws are perceived as maintaining the structure of our nation and its values. Yet this concept may come into conflict with that of the value of human life, and so the original vision of persons as ends becomes entangled and hidden in the maintenance of the system. At Stage 3, the interpretation, simplistically stated, has become, "The good person is concerned about the value of human life." But a conflict is raised when one is confronted with a "bad" person who is not concerned about the value of all human life. Need one be concerned about such a person? Despite these conflicts, the shaping vision brings its biting edge into all the stages, raising questions about point of view. Thus the vision can act as powerful content at any stage.

In the same way, religious traditions embody visions in their literature, law, rituals, and other symbols. And again the vision can be hidden by the very forms that have attempted to give it body and substance. Church or religious law, designed to give substance to the vision, may replace the vision. So the vision or shaping process needs to become a part of the content, experienced in ways that can be appropriated at each stage.

Fowler has described symbols at Stage 6 as transparent to the depth of the actuality which they represent, shaped and regenerated by the experience of the individual.[10] Taking that idea as a vision, we need to consider a continual reclarifying of our own understandings if we are to allow our symbols to shape and reshape the depths of our relationships and our journey.

Educational implications and ways of helping the vision to perform its shaping function will be explored in subsequent chapters.

QUIZ

Thinking about Stage 6 is a very reflective activity if we are concerned about the vision it may represent. One way to reflect on its implications is to engage in the following exercise.

1. Have paper and pencil on hand.

2. Think about one value in your life which is so important that you feel as if you would never change your mind about it.

3. Draw a picture or symbol representing that value.

4. Explore how this value relates to the impressions of the shaping vision presented in this chapter.

5. Explore: Does this kind of comparison offer some ideas about how you might reshape your value to some extent?

6. Try talking about this value to a child and to another adult. Think about what you guess might be happening to your own understandings and to those of the persons with whom you are talking.

CHAPTER IX
The Real Person

INTRODUCTION

Pete is a lively eighth grader who has always been a good student. He was interviewed and scored for logical and moral reasoning and was found to be primarily concrete-operational and at Stage 2 in moral reasoning. Recently in social studies, the class has been taking an overview of a series of historical events, working back into time from the present. Pete has no problem understanding that he is thirteen years old in this particular year A.D., but he can make no sensible connections between that fact and the mixture of names, dates, and places that confront him each day in class.

Sue is a thirty-five-year-old wife and mother back in graduate school and is struggling with difficult decisions about a disintegrating marriage and a new career focus. She is formal-operational, primarily Stage 3 with some Stage 2 moral reasoning. In her attempt to make some sense out of her situation, one of her urgent pleas is: "I want to hear some good examples from history and society about what responsibility means."

Jenny is trying to establish herself in a profession that has been traditionally male dominated. She is highly formal-operational, consistently Stage 5 in moral reasoning. She spends many sleepless nights trying to figure out how she can communicate her convictions without being a threat to others, without damaging the cause of women within her chosen profession, and yet speaking and acting in ways that are consistent with her beliefs.

These three brief descriptions give us glimpses of real persons with challenges, problems, feelings, decisions, and methods for trying to make sense and meaning out of their lives. How can we relate cognitive developmental theory to these people without labeling them? How can we recognize other aspects of their personalities and respect their unique qualities? How can we relate theory to behavior and actual decision-making? In this chapter I will deal with these questions under the following subheadings:

—A Model or Theory Isn't a Person

—Labeling, Oversimplification, and Jumping to Conclusions or Misuse of Theory

—Moral Reasoning and Behavior

—Decision-Making and The Shaping Vision

A MODEL OR THEORY ISN'T A PERSON

A model is something like a map; it represents a real entity, but is not the same thing as the reality. Early maps were strikingly inaccurate in many ways, yet they served to help travelers find their way about. As more precise measuring devices have been developed, maps have become increasingly accurate representations of the land surfaces. When discrepancies occur, the map is checked and altered; one would not consider changing the land area in order to fit the map!

In a similar way, the description of the six stages is a map or model, an attempt to represent how people think. As persons have been interviewed using moral dilemmas, patterns of how they reason have emerged. When the same persons have been interviewed repeatedly over a period of years (a longitudinal study), sequences of patterning have become apparent. These patterns have been organized into the stages of Kohlberg's theory. His model is derived from real people, but must never be confused with the reality of the actual individuals themselves. We do not attempt to shape persons to fit into the stages; rather, the model is altered when there are discrepancies between it and new information about human thinking processes.

Accompanying this structural model are attempts to explain *why* people develop such structures and how cognitive development relates to other models. In this way a theory of cognitive structural development has emerged. From the beginning it has been questioned, challenged, examined and reexamined, refined, and altered. It is a living, changing creation, pulsating with the infinite complexities of human minds that are both its building blocks and its creators.

MISUSE OF THEORY OR LABELING, OVERSIMPLIFICATION, AND JUMPING TO CONCLUSIONS

An unfortunate misuse of this theory has been to perceive it as a static and simplistic structure that can be laid on people who can then be pulled around and reformed so that they fit neatly into the stage boxes. Such hazardous use of the model seems to result from too brief an exposure to the material or from the inability or unwillingness to delve into it responsibly. One of the major purposes of this book is to make clear the complexity of the subject and to discourage its simplistic appropriation. This problem will be considered throughout this section.

A second misuse of the theory is to assign value to persons according to the stage at which they have been scored. Because higher stages are more complex and provide tools for dealing with complex situations, it is easy to fall into the trap of considering people who reason at higher stages to be "better" than those who are at lower stages. Structural developmental theory can be used to dehumanize and manipulate in a destructive sense, or it can be used in the service of realizing human potential. But the latter use also raises serious ethical questions.

To elaborate, in our culture it is unacceptable for a child to be allowed to starve or to be physically abused. When this occurs, government steps in and assumes responsibility so that the child may grow to normal physical adulthood. We are imbued with the conviction that each person has a basic right to normal development in the physical sense, that it is better to have a healthy whole body than one that is handicapped by illness or deformity, or that is stunted in growth. My children have all had to wear glasses since early childhood. In no way does this make them less acceptable as persons, but it has put certain limitations on them. If the technology were available to give each person perfect eyesight, few of us would consider it unethical to offer it. Yet, in contrast, we often react quite differently to cognitive developmental theory. We often perceive the attempt to stimulate cognitive or moral reasoning as interfering with the rights of individuals to remain as they are. This reaction is due in part to the newness of the idea and in part to justifiable fears of labeling others or implying that they are not wholly acceptable. Our hesitancy is a wise precaution, yet these theories say that human development follows a potential sequence. Movement through this sequence is made possible through stimulation of cognitive conflict by challenges raised from a stage just ahead of wherever one is. When the cognitive conflict is unavailable, unperceived, or rejected, then movement through the sequence ceases.

As already stated, persons prefer the highest stage they can understand and reject lower-stage reasoning. The more complex the thinking processes, the more options are open to the individual in solving problems, making decisions, and understanding one's world. The higher the stage, the more possibilities there are for a person to deal with the complexities of life. So we are caught in the tension between accepting persons where they are, respecting their rights and individuality, and, on the other hand, choosing to support OR to deprive persons of opportunities for development. Do we accept limitations?

Do we attempt to improve eyesight when the means are available?

There is no simplistic answer. All education is actually intervention into the lives of those being educated. Perhaps the ethical question is not, "Should we introduce cognitive conflict?" but, "Can we ethically decide to deprive an individual of the opportunity to grow in a manner and at a pace most appropriate for that individual?" The very real danger in the use of developmental theory is that it can be used to achieve a teacher's or parent's limited goals for the student or child. The person then becomes subservient to the purposes of others, and ultimately the means to some externally chosen end. As Kohlberg has pointed out: "Morality based on the principle of justice. . . . 'is not fanatical; it does not sacrifice other persons to one's own beliefs and ideals.' "[1]

In general, use of developmental theory might be seen in terms of opening doors, of holding out the carrot, rather than shoving people through doors or cramming the carrot down their throats. As I shall discuss in the next chapter, the implications for the education of children and youth may be quite different from those for adults.

The complexities of the thinking of any individual, even the youngest child, preclude simplistic judgments in terms of stages. If we refer back to Pete, Sue, and Jenny mentioned earlier in this chapter, we notice that Sue does not completely fit into any of the descriptions defining the stages. She is formal operational and partly conventional (Stage 3), but is also partly preconventional (Stage 2). The spread of Sue's thinking is somewhat broader than the average span, but we have found that very few individuals fit neatly into one category. For instance, most adults we have interviewed have straddled Stages 3 and 4 in moral reasoning, some using more 3 than 4, some more 4 than 3. Some appear to be more formal operational than others, although we have not done precise testing in that area. Occasionally we have found individuals who use three adjacent stages, either 2, 3, and 4 or 3, 4, and 5. (Fowler's faith stages closely parallel moral reasoning stages, but there are variations also between models.)

In order to obtain a valid score for an individual, it is essential to use a series of dilemmas such as those constituting Form A, as each one touches on different issues. (See Appendix A for the dilemmas and questions.) The quotations I have used in this book come from the first research project in which we used an older form of the Heinz dilemma (III) and in which we were only looking for responses to the issues of punishment and the value of life. This older form of the dilemma is now incorporated into Dilemmas III and III' as given in the appendix. Our current research uses these two plus Dilemma I in order to obtain complete scores for the persons interviewed. Dilemma I centers on the issues of contract and authority, with responses scored in the following areas of focus:
—why a promise should be kept
—bases for ownership of property
—the meaning of a father's authority
—affiliation: the relationship between father and son
Each of these areas is understood in a different way at each stage. For instance—It is important to keep a promise:

Stage 1: because if you don't you get punished.

Stage 2: so that the other person will keep a promise to you.

Stage 3: so that others won't form a bad impression of you.
in order to have a good and lasting relationship.

Stage 4: because otherwise order in the society is disrupted.
because a promise is a pact or formal statement.

Stage 5: because this affirms the worth or dignity of the other person.[2]

This is an abbreviated list of responses and does not do justice to the complexity of the replies. But it may be helpful to the reader to see how different issues can relate to the stages of social perspective already described and to become aware of other issues that have been given little treatment in this book.

Another aspect of scoring involves the modes or moral decision-making strategies described in chapter 4. To recap, the first two modes are "standards" and "simple consequences." Both of these tend to consider a situation in a limited way and are termed "situation-bound." When used at any stage, this is designated by an "A," for instance, 2A or 4A, and is called a substage. The second two modes, "justice" and "conscience or perfectionism," tend to be more inclusive, reversible, and balanced, and are designated "B" substage. Both substages probably function at all stages, although there is some question about their relationship to Stage 5. Kohlberg says:

Our longitudinal data indeed support the notion that the two types are relatively clear substages. The B substage is more mature than the A substage in the sense that a 3A may move to 3B, but a 3B can never move to 3A (though he may move to 4A). Individuals can skip the B substage, that is, move from 3A to 4A; but if they change substage, it is always from A to B. In a sense, then, the B substage is a consolidation or equilibration of the social perspective first elaborated at the A substage. B's are more balanced in perspective.[3]

The substages are distinguished in the scoring manual and become a part of the scoring process. Their value may not be apparent to the reader and to introduce them here may seem confusing rather than clarifying. However, I consider it important that anyone involved in using these developmental theories be fully aware of the complexities inherent in them. Initial confusion and humility are more conducive to ultimately responsible use than confidence based in an overly simplistic understanding! It is a privilege to enter into the complex structure of individual human minds where each idea, each way of thinking, is a source of wonder and respect. There may be glimpses of tentative groping toward new structures while the individual struggles to cling to old structures.

One is ever amazed at the intricacies of the human mind. Again and again one may be struck with the realization that models can never express the true complexity and beauty of any individual mind as it thinks and reasons and tries to make sense out of what is experienced and perceived. Perhaps my major hope for this book is that it may enable the reader to approach each individual with a new awareness and appreciation for what it means to be a person.

An important way of relating cognitive structural developmental theory to the whole person is through an understanding of its relationship to other models and theories. There is then a temptation to draw parallels among different theories, but I have found this to be very risky, even when one is well informed concerning the models involved. Jane Loevinger explores relationships among a number of developmental theories in her book, *Ego Development*.[4] This is a good source of information for the reader who is interested in pursuing the subject further. Here I quote from her conclusions:

Every classification is an injustice, . . . The injustice is compounded in lining up the stages of one psychologist's system with those of another. The authors whose schemes have been reviewed are not all talking about the same variable all the time, but in all the expositions there are some common elements, common phenomena to which they give varying access. The cumulative effect is that there is some underlying reality. Moreover, having found as many versions as we have in as many places, we cannot doubt that there are many more. Summarizing the correspondence of stages and types, may do more harm than good, since they encourage premature closure on complex issues. There is no way to say exactly what stage or type in one system corresponds with that of another.

For the benefit of anyone who might be tempted to make any developmental theory an absolute or simplistic model, I want to repeat Loevinger's statement that such an approach limits our vision by encouraging "premature closure on complex issues."

MORAL REASONING AND BEHAVIOR

Earlier in the book I stressed the necessity of distinguishing between moral reasoning and behavior (or thinking and acting). Now we can take a look at the whole person—What are the behavioral implications of moral reasoning for a person? We have already mentioned a number of factors that go into making decisions and these will be explored further in the next section. What we are interested in here is how moral reasoning might influence decision-making and ultimately behavior, in other words, relationships between stage of moral reasoning and behavior.

There is only limited information available to us in answer to these questions and additional insight awaits further research. To start off, let us refer again to the Heinz dilemma and the question, *Should Heinz steal the drug?* In the introduction to the scoring manual we find this information:

To some extent, the individual's stage generates a probability of choice on this dilemma. Roughly speaking, about 90 percent of Stage 1 subjects think it wrong to steal; about 90 percent of Stage 5 subjects think it right. Choice, however, is not in itself a good guide to stage. Although one can, with some probability, predict choice from stage, one cannot predict stage from choice. While 90 percent of Stage 5 subjects think it right to steal, so do about 90 percent of Stage 2 subjects, 70 percent of Stage 3 subjects, and 50 percent of Stage 4 subjects.[5]

Therefore, all we can deduce from such data is a fair probability of predicting choice from stage. *We cannot predict stage from choice.* In other words, a person's choice and resultant behavior is no indication of stage! But this leads us to the subsequent question: How well can we predict behavior from stage?

In a study of undergraduate students, reported in 1967, almost half of the conventional subjects cheated while only 11 percent of those using postconventional reasoning did so.[6] In another study, Richard Krebs and Lawrence

Kohlberg found that there was increasing *resistance* to cheating, from 30 percent at the **Preconventional Level** to 80 percent at the **Postconventional Level.**[7] There was some indication in the study that preconventional subjects went through no battle of conscience and that when there was a decision not to cheat it was based on their perception of practical, external factors. They did not clearly differentiate between moral and nonmoral factors. Stage 3 students were particularly susceptible to pressures to cheat when "everyone else does it," and they tended to place major emphasis on motivation or intention. This confirms what we heard in our interviews: "Breaking the law is all right as long as it is helping someone."

Guilt, that bad feeling in the pit of the stomach, may be experienced at all stages, but its sources are different. For instance, at Stage 1, the source may be fear of punishment; at Stage 3, fear of disapproval and loss of face; at Stage 5, the sinking feeling that arises from not living up to one's own principles. Emotional intensity may be the same, but "the difference is a real one, . . . since intense fear of punishment does not predict a resistance to temptation, whereas self-critical guilt does."[8]

Dan Candee's research into the moral issues of Watergate suggests that one explanation for the actions of the participants is that "the Watergate actors can be seen as morally confused rather than morally malicious."[9] Candee writes: ". . . . the participants were enthusiastic but essentially ordinary people who responded to the pressures of the campaign with decisions that from a stage 3 or 4 point of view seemed right or at least permissible."

He points out how the concept of basic rights, perceived as the central issue from a Stage 5 viewpoint, becomes simply a virtue at Stage 3 in competition with other virtues such as loyalty and truthfulness. At Stage 3 and 4, the action of any legitimate authority may be seen as legitimate in itself, and thus all other actors in the situation are relieved of responsibility. From a Stage 5 perspective, personal responsibility takes on ultimate significance, and we would expect more predictability as this stage is founded in a sense of personal integrity and universal rights. At the Conventional Level (Stage 3 or 4), it would seem that behavior might be predicted to the extent of one's beliefs based in significant personal and institutional relationships. Lickona has written that

in fact, to be consistent with Stage 3 or 4 conventional moral principles, it is *necessary* to be "inconsistent"—to vary one's behavior to conform to the changing situational definition of the right thing to do. At Stage 5, prediction of behavioral choice in a resistance-to-temptation situation is easier, since cheating is difficult to reconcile with postconventional considerations of honoring and maintaining equality with other test-takers. In other situations, however, the choice for a Stage 5 person is less clear-cut—as when two principled values such as social contract and respect for the rights of others are in conflict.[10]

Kohlberg writes:

In summary, then, while moral judgment maturity is only one of many predictors of action in moral conflict situations, it can be quite a powerful and meaningful predictor of action where it gives rise to distinctive ways of defining concrete situational rights and duties in socially ambiguous situations. The causal role of moral judgment appears to be due to its contribution to a "cognitive" definition of the situation. . . .[11]

Simply put, one's moral stage determines to a great extent how one perceives the issues in a situation, both in terms of which issues are recognized and how they are seen in terms of priority. In the next section, we will look at decision-making as a process and the way this relates to developmental theory.

DECISION-MAKING AND THE SHAPING VISION

Pete, Sue, and Jenny are all caught in situations in which they may choose among alternatives—helplessness, impetuous action, or rational decision-making.

Pete, limited by his logical reasoning level to concrete operations, is going to have difficulty generating options. Even hard study is not going to overcome his concrete-operational inability to understand historical time. Sue can hypothesize alternatives, but left to her own resources she is not going to be able to include societal standards and universal values in her decision-making. Jenny may be overwhelmed by the complexity of her situation as she struggles with its many facets. As she sits in meetings making critical decisions with her professional peers, she may find herself dominated by others who are more vocal and perhaps more opinionated.

It is my suggestion that we look at formal operations and postconventional perspective for clues that might enable these persons to make responsible decisions. In this way, I believe we can derive a shaping vision for decision-making that can be made concrete as a practical procedure. Pulling qualities from formal operations and postconventional perspective, I propose the following ingredients for decision-making:

—the generation of a maximum number of alternatives
—the identification of a maximum number of issues
—methods of putting issues, moral and otherwise, into an order of priority
—respect for the rights of all persons involved, treating persons as ends rather than means
—methods for testing the validity of hypotheses/ alternatives

In the process of decision-making we need to take into account that the individuals making decisions are whole persons with differing feelings, points of view, and ways of making meaning out of the world in general and therefore out of specific situations.

In order to most effectively carry out such a procedure, it is best engaged in within a community. This community may consist of one other trusted individual, or a family, committee, class, or some other group. In these settings the decisions to be made may be those of one indi-

vidual or of the collective community. Only in community is it ordinarily possible to generate a maximum number
of alternative ideas and solutions and to test out
conclusions.

In Pete's situation, the process might be initiated with
parents, teacher, and/or school counselor, with qualified
adults carrying the responsibility for directing the
process since Pete's grasp of the overall procedure will be
limited. Sue and Jenny will need to identify their
respective "communities" as they work toward solutions
for their personal problems. But since Jenny is involved
with professional decision-making groups, she may be
able to introduce elements of the process into the
meetings, as this approach has proven to be very effective
in conflict situations. The steps might be as follows:

1. Brainstorm everyone's concerns about the problem
or issue, making a visible list on chalkboard or large
paper. This method usually elicits a good number of the
group's concerns and allows persons to express feelings.
In brainstorming, all ideas are accepted and no value
judgments are made. Writing out ideas accomplishes at
least two things: it makes clear that each person's ideas
have been heard and considered, and it separates ideas
from personalities. Especially in situations where there is
strong disagreement, it helps to free the subsequent
discussion of ideas from attacks on people.

2. Formulate a tentative statement of the issue—what
is the group really talking about? This is not as easy as it
sounds for individuals invariably bring quite different
conceptions of the issue to a discussion. This step also
involves defining terms because its purpose is to clarify
the issues. For instance, as Pete and his teacher talk
further, they may find that for Pete the problem is a feeling
of inadequacy and helplessness, while for the teacher it is
that Pete does not appear to be doing his homework.
Getting out these concerns helps to formulate the real
issue—What can be done to help Pete cope with his
inability to grasp historical time?

3. Organize the concerns from Steps 1 and 2 into a few major categories. Some of the categories may be clearly practical, some moral, some emotional. Others might be theological, or aesthetic. Sorting these may aid in further clarifying the issue or issues.

4. Look for information related to these categories. Determine whether the data gathered are facts, or opinions and value judgments, and how they are relevant to the issue. For example, Pete's teacher may decide to find out more about Pete's learning abilities by consulting with his other teachers. One of them thinks that Pete is slow. His teacher decides that this is a value judgment. She then goes to his test scores, which reveal among many other things that he is musically talented and concrete-operational. His musical ability is probably not relevant to the issue at hand, but the concrete-operational score may well be.

5. If there are several categories of concerns, rank them according to the priority they should take in the making of a decision. In the case of Pete, there is little complication. But in many decisions issues and concerns are very complex. For instance, in Sue's case of family and career uncertainties, she will probably have to look at practical concerns (such as finances), moral concerns (her commitment to marriage, or family), and emotional concerns (of self, children, husband, and other family members).

6. Make a tentative decision and test run the idea. Some testing questions that might be asked are:
   a. Does the decision reflect the concerns and priorities of individual group members who are involved in the decision?
   b. If the basis for the decision is stated as a principle and universally applied to similar situations, is it a fair solution?
   c. Putting yourself in the place of each person in the situation, do you consider the solution a fair one for all involved? (This is Stage 6 ideal role-taking. It is further described as an exercise in chapter 11.)

In reflecting on this decision-making process in light of cognitive structural development, some limitations become apparent. For instance, the individual whose logical reasoning is concrete-operational may not be able to generate alternate ways of solving a problem and may have difficulty coping with too great a variety of alternatives suggested by others. Group processing is an excellent way to suggest other points of view, but it may also be confusing to a concrete-operational way of thinking.

In addition, limited role-taking ability may make it difficult to attribute validity to the concerns of others, which in turn restricts the assembling of information because at some stages certain aspects of the problem seem irrelevant to the issue. At the **Preconventional** and **Conventional Levels** there is also a tendency to see any statement that is part of one's own world-view as a fact of life. For instance, the statement "Stealing is wrong because it is taking from somebody" was perceived as a statement of fact by one of our interviewees. Its opposite, "Stealing is right when it is helping somebody" was also seen as fact by another conventional thinker. The first individual was thrown into confusion by this contradiction. This example is representative of an apparent inconsistency that is almost insoluble through concrete operations and Stage 3 moral reasoning.

Since the attempt to formulate a principle for testing purposes is a function of formal operations and post-conventional reasoning, this step will not be understood at other levels. Testing by means of role-taking and the application of a principle are additional tasks that require cognitive complexity.[12]

Identifying the limitations in this process suggested for making decisions helps us to see that we are dealing with "a shaping vision." Many of us find ourselves in positions—classrooms, counseling situations, committees—where we are in some sense responsible for decision-making processes. It is an exciting challenge to keep a vision in mind, to use it in sensitive and supportive ways, allowing it to shape the way that people experience making decisions even before the experience can be fully understood. This decision-making process is a democratic procedure, one that is based on the concerns of all the individuals involved, but which also utilizes *informed* opinion. I think it is consistent with the vision of the founders of our Constitution and with the intent of the decision-making structures of many other institutions, including churches. It is an example of the process that forms the basis for "the just community" as described in the next chapter.

SUMMARY

In this chapter I have attempted to bring together cognitive structural developmental theory and the real person, to focus on some of the implications that this model has for what it means to be a whole person. Cognitive developmental theory is one window, and I maintain, an important window into how humans understand their world and find meaning within it. Its complexity and the complexity of each individual preclude easy correlations with other theories. Serious ethical questions must be considered about how this theory is to be used in respect to persons. Emotional components are intertwined with the values that form the basis for each stage, which may block or facilitate movement to higher stages. Strong emotion can obscure rational functions, but it can also support high commitment to chosen values.

Decision-making may be influenced by many factors. I would suggest the following formula to express what enters into a decision: issue(s) + emotions + practical considerations + moral reasoning + ego strength = decision(s). It seems that moral reasoning assumes greater control over decision-making at higher stages.

There are implications in this for social and political

issues. Some of these have been suggested in quotes from Mylai and Watergate participants. I would now like to bring this aspect into clear focus. I have previously briefly described responses to questions based on Matthew 12:9-14. One of the questions posed in that research project was: *Were the Pharisees justified in being upset with Jesus because he broke their law?*

The results of the research showed that persons whose moral reasoning was scored at Stages 1, 2, and 3, saw no reason (particularly at Stages 2 and 3) for the Pharisees to be upset because Jesus was helping somebody or doing good. But for those who were scored at Stage 4, there was an understanding of the position of the Pharisees which the subjects explained in the following ways:

Jesus posed a very definite threat to the stability of their society.

. . . because of their background . . . in respect that this is a law that they were supposed to uphold.

. . . they had to answer to their society. You've got to understand that they have their own standards, and I suppose by their standards you just flat should not break the law.

We find here expressions of an understanding of the structure of society and of responsibility in terms of civic roles. What the results clearly appear to suggest is that the social perspective or world-view of persons scored at Stages 1, 2, and 3 did not allow them to take the role of persons (the Pharisees) whose world-view included a major concern for maintaining the structure of society.

Quotations already given from some of the Watergate participants demonstrate how social perspective influenced behavior in that specific situation. Such evidence suggests all sorts of questions about participation in government and other institutions. Our nation was built on the concept of an educated citizenry able to make responsible decisions through participatory democracy. If much of our adult population is unable to get inside a Stage 4 institutional perspective; if only a small percentage is able to participate with awareness and under-standing in the democratic process and comprehend the relationships among the different branches of govern-ment, does this not help to explain some of the misuses of governmental authority by political figures?

How does this affect the aims of education for public schools and for the teaching of democratic concepts at different ages? If most high school students hold a social perspective of Stage 3 or lower, how can democracy be taught so that it will have meaning for the student at his or her present level and will also stimulate movement toward the shaping vision of our Constitution?

One can raise similar questions about the teaching of religion. How does one communicate a vision to help shape understandings for the present without fixing them in distorted forms that may then be carried for life?

The next three chapters explore some educational implications of cognitive developmental theory.

QUIZ

Here is a brief review quiz for Chapter 9. Match the statements in Column A with the answers in Column B.

Column A	Column B
1. A model represents something real, but _____	1. living, changing creation.
2. The theory of structural development is a _____	2. is not the same thing as the reality.
3. Theories of structural development suggest that there is _____	3. formal operations and a postconventional perspective.
4. A real danger in the use of developmental theory is that it might be used to _____	4. irresponsible use and premature closure on complex issues.
5. The majority of adults interviewed reason at stages _____	5. a potential sequence for all humans.
6. A simplistic understanding of developmental theory can lead to _____	6. 3 and 4.
7. Behavior is not an indication of _____	7. stage.
8. A shaping vision in decision-making might be derived from _____	8. sacrifice others in the service of one's own beliefs.

ANSWERS
1. 2 2. 1 3. 5 4. 8 5. 6 6. 4 7. 7 8. 3

CHAPTER X
Values, Development, and Education

INTRODUCTION

In the last chapter I raised some questions that I consider critical in formulating aims for secular and religious education. How can we enable persons, young or old, to appropriate the visions that can shape our societies, our faiths, and our lives according to the highest values we have available to us? How does cognitive developmental theory inform our answers to this question? Based in an understanding of the person as a whole entity, what else do we need to consider?

Before I answer these questions directly, I would like to reflect on three currently common responses made by educational institutions to the contemporary concern about values. These were described in chapter 1, but I shall repeat them here:

1. Leave values education to the home and church.
2. Teach the traditional values on which everyone agrees.
3. Help each person to discover what his or her own values are, making no judgments about them.

After briefly evaluating each of these responses, I shall describe a fourth option, an educational model that takes seriously both developmental theory and the whole person. I will then lift out for closer inspection some selected aspects of developmental education: the stimulation of development and some ethical distinctions among approaches to children, youth, and adults.

In chapter 11 I will suggest and describe actual strategies for implementing this model, emphasizing those that stimulate development.

THREE CONTEMPORARY RESPONSES

Each of the following responses has important contributions to make in the development of persons, but each also has serious shortcomings. I will be pointing out both positive and negative features of each response in this very brief critique.

RESPONSE 1: Leave values education to the home and church.

This response by a school system is a valid one in that much values education does and should go on in homes and religious institutions. The fallacy in the argument, however, is that it disregards the fact that values education goes on constantly in the schools, whether or not we are aware of it. For instance, the teacher who insists on neat papers and orderly desks is teaching that neatness is a positive value. Or, the teacher who rewards "good" behavior with gold stars or extra privileges is demonstrating that that particular type of behavior carries high value. I put the word "good" in quotation marks because the connotation of "good" can vary greatly among teachers. For instance, my children were downgraded by some teachers for not following directions exactly; they were rewarded by others for finding new and creative ways of doing their work.

I observed a broader example of values being implicitly taught in the schools when I attended an orientation program for incoming tenth graders. The program devoted one hour and a half to descriptions of athletic programs and plugs for pep club activities. Announcements of all other activities and scholastic opportunities were crammed into twenty minutes at the end of the evening. This proportion turned out to be a realistic expression of the priorities and values that functioned in that school.

At another level, states express their educational values when they set standards for which school districts are held accountable. Testing procedures are set up which stress some kinds of academic achievement to the exclusion of other kinds of learning. In reaction to the options offered by school systems, we see the creation of "alternative" schools by students and parents whose values differ from these standards of learning. Educational values are evident in "back-to-the-basics" views which may conflict with those in humanistic education.

These are examples of values that may be inherent in different schools and school systems. Yet these same schools may reject any "values program" on the basis that public schools cannot or should not teach values. I contend that there is no such thing as "value-free education" and that administrators, teachers, parents, and students need to be aware of what values are being taught and what the outcomes might be for the students.

RESPONSE 2: Teach the traditional values on which everyone agrees.

This response is sometimes called "the character education approach," in which certain selected virtues are taught and "caught." On first consideration, it might seem that we could all agree on such virtues as honesty, service, self-control, loyalty, reverence, cleanliness, obedience, and bravery. However, a brief reflection on the difficulties of Watergate and Mylai participants in relationship to loyalty and obedience points up the problems. A major difficulty with this approach is that it is not possible for persons to agree upon interpretations and therefore upon an acceptable list of virtues. These qualities, called a "bag of virtues" by Kohlberg, are often considered to be universal values. But the varieties of meanings attributed to them, and the fact that they cannot be applied consistently in all situations, precludes their universality.

A second major difficulty, discouraging to proponents of this approach, is that *learning* any particular set of values does not significantly influence behavior. An early study of moral character, conducted by Hartshorne and May in the United States in the late 1920s, included honesty, service, and self-control as the character traits studied.[1] They discovered, as have other researchers since, that the world simply cannot be divided into honest and dishonest people. Almost everyone cheats some of the time, depending on individual situations. And "people who cheat express as much or more disapproval of cheating as those who do not cheat." Kohlberg also found that

vices and virtues do have a central significance to individuals at the conventional level of morality; our praise and blame of others is based on ascribing virtues and vices to them. At the preconventional level, virtues and vices have no such significance because the individual does not care about intention. . . . At the stage of moral principle [Postconventional Level], the individual is oriented towards acting to create a moral state of affairs, not towards "being honest."[2]

In the same article, Kohlberg suggests that vices and virtues, praise and blame, are "necessary parts of moral development, but should not be used to define its ends."[3] And in Response 2, that is where a major problem lies, in that its *ultimate* purpose is the teaching of selected virtues.

Again, we can see valuable use of this response in the light of developmental theory, but both this theory and other research point out its serious limitations.

RESPONSE 3: Help each person to discover what his or her own values are, making no judgments about them.

This response is primarily relativistic in that each person is granted freedom to believe whatever he or she wants. This option is currently a very popular one, generally implemented by what is called "values clarification." Values clarification is attractive to public schools because on the surface it avoids any connotation of values inculcation that might be objectionable to some students and parents. It has caught on quickly in religious education and in other settings, probably because it is often fun and interesting for participants, is considered easy to use, and promotes good discussion. It is making a significant contribution to the whole education scene, but I think that it needs to be used with care and judgment and in the context of broader educational goals. I raise the following concerns about its use:

1. Rather than being "value-free," such relativism is simply a different kind of absolutism in which it is unacceptable to make any judgments about the values of others and set standards against which one may check one's own values. It is a matter of what seems good and right to each individual. I raise the question: Might not a steady dose of such relativism reinforce Stage 2 "do-your-own-thing" structures and Stage 3 stereotypes absorbed from a relativistic culture or subculture? Many adolescents demonstrate such an orientation. What in this approach will help to stimulate adolescents toward Stage 4 reasoning? An interesting speculation can be made about what might happen to a Stage 4 perspective if the standards of our culture dissolved into complete tolerance. At that point might not the system disintegrate into anarchy? I believe that "value-free" is in itself a powerful value that may well aggravate disciplinary and learning problems in schools.

2. A second concern involves the responsibility of the teacher in relation to values expressed by the students. If a group of sixth graders decides that it is all right to lie about one's age in order to get into a movie more cheaply, should the teacher simply accept that conclusion? It is possible that there may be children who do not agree, but who are unable to stand up against the peer pressure exerted by the vocal students, or the majority. Will silence on the part of the teacher suggest acceptance and approval of the students' values? It seems that the professional or parent who uses values clarification strategies needs to consider carefully his or her own understanding of its goals and results.

3. Values clarification strategies are used frequently as games and gimmicks. They are fun at first because students enjoy the freedom of discussion that they

engender. However, increasingly there are reports from teachers that students are saying, "Oh, we've already done that." or "I don't see the point of that." They are bored with "values" because the strategies are used without the broad concern of gradual development and without an anchor in subject matter relevant to students.

On the other hand, some strategies arouse powerful emotions. The teacher or leader who is unaware of this or who is not prepared to handle emotional responses may be unable to help students in constructive and supportive ways.

Values clarification strategies are one of the most useful teaching techniques I have discovered, as I shall elaborate in chapter 11. Properly utilized, they can stimulate reasoning; they can open up discussion; they can help persons to express feelings; they can facilitate listening and communication within a group. But they have doubtful value when used without an understanding of their limitations.

A FOURTH RESPONSE: A MODEL FOR TEACHING THE WHOLE PERSON

Developmental theory as described in this book suggests to us that we cannot teach values in isolation from other aspects of the individual's understanding. As educators, our primary concern is to focus on how individual persons make sense and meaning out of what they experience, how their world-views are constructed, and how this affects their everyday lives.

I am going to share two incidents that I think concisely demonstrate two completely different approaches to education and learning.

Incident 1: At age five Janie taught Carlie, who was four, to give the right answers to the interviewer. She told Carlie the clay balls contained the same amount of clay and that the pieces "just looked different when one was smashed." It was not until the interviewer changed the clay shapes from balls to snakes that Carlie's lack of comprehension of conservation of amount became apparent. Carlie had appropriated some factual knowledge, but she was not able to apply it to other situations, and she was unaware that she did not really understand the subject at all!

Incident 2: When Janie worked through the problem of conservation with the clay balls, (as described in chapters 2 and 3), she struggled with physical discrepancies, which from her own experience did not fit with her mental images. In this process she constructed a new view of reality, a more complex and adequate way of understanding her world: that of concrete operations.

Carlie's experience, in incident 1, demonstrates the most common approach to education, the transmission of knowledge, be it scientific fact, abstract ideas, or moral values. The character education approach, described as Response 2 in this chapter, is another example of this concept of teaching.

Janie's experience, however, exemplifies a different approach growing out of the conviction that each individual is born with the potential to develop, to construct his or her own world-views, and to make meaning out of such world-views. These constructions involve active participation in the process and cannot be poured into the head as water might be poured into an empty container. Janie had "poured" information into Carlie's head, it occupied space as an X but it made no connections with the way Carlie's mind had put her world together.

If we are concerned with teaching/learning as the development of individual world-and-meaning constructions rather than as the transmission and reception of information, I suggest that we need to look at six major elements basic to this kind of learning:

(1) Information must be available to the learner to be acted upon, to be assimilated by the structure, and at times to cause change or accommodation in the structure itself. It is the responsibility of the instructor, whether

this be parent or teacher, to provide the stuff for the learner to act upon. This stuff may be spelling words, building blocks, religious concepts, water and mud, books, or mathematical formulae, offered in such ways that the learner can interact with it/them. After the individual has acted on this stuff, it becomes content in his or her brain structure. This content of learning may be facts, information, values, ideas, and skills important to a culture or religious tradition. Developmental theory tells us that content will be interpreted differently at different stages. This first element is called significant content.

(2) The instructor needs to be aware of the manifestations of developmental theory in terms of how the learner is interpreting and appropriating important content and for the stimulation or pacing of development through the use of content and methodology. This kind of awareness assists the instructor in deciding what content is appropriate, how it might be presented in ways consistent with the student's structuring, and suggests ways for developing communication among instructor, content, and learner.

(3) It is my assumption that each person is an emotional being, and that feelings play a critical role in learning. Any educational approach needs to take this into account and to help students learn how to use their emotions constructively in the learning process.[4]

(4) Contemporary research shows us that the human mind functions not only in a rational, analytical, verbal, and logical way, but also has a generally less respected and neglected set of functions: imagination, creativity, synthesis, analogy and metaphor, intuition, and mental images. The rational functions seem to be performed more commonly by the left hemisphere of the brain, and the imagistic by the right hemisphere. For maximum efficiency in learning, both kinds of functions need to be engaged.[5]

(5) The learner seems to require active physical involvement for optimum learning to take place. Manip-

ulating clay balls is one example, and how many of us find that underlining and outlining help us to fix ideas in the mind when reading? It appears that the simple physical act of using the pencil is a part of this process. This way of learning or representing has been labeled "enactive."[6] Enactive learning encompasses many kinds of activities: writing, drawing, role-playing, dramatizing, building with blocks. Enactive activities may include emotions and right and left brain functions, but the physical experience is a highly significant dimension.

(6) Learning is facilitated by the support of a community which may be a family, peer group, classroom, school, or church. The supporting community can help each person feel accepted as an individual of value, while providing a setting for the developing person to explore new ways of thinking, to make mistakes, and to try out new forms of behavior. Without this community, the individual may feel timid, or "different" and isolated, and growth may be stifled.

In order to demonstrate these six elements in a concrete way, let us refer back to the simple interviews with Janie and the learning she achieved as she played with the clay balls. In this example, the interviewer functioned in the role of teacher.

We note that first the teacher provided the stuff or resources of learning (the clay), the instructions, and the knowledge of the subject matter (conservation of amount). In other words, this was not an unstructured session based on "What do you want to do today?" Rather, it was a well-planned setting for learning appropriate content and with specific goals in mind. The developmental potential was clear to the teacher, as was the use of techniques to stimulate it.

The "right" answer was not given by the teacher because this might have retarded learning rather than stimulate it. However, when Janie made statements contrary to the facts that she could understand ("I put the clay over there"), the teacher did not simply accept this.

191

She expressed her own point of view, her own observations ("I didn't see you do that"), and she raised questions. This stimulated cognitive conflict in Janie, but did not devalue her ideas. The teacher was aware of the emotional involvement that Janie had invested in the situation and respected this attachment, both for the sake of Janie's feelings at that moment, and in recognition that too much threat or disapproval can cut off learning. The teacher here functioned as the community of support for the child.

Janie was encouraged to handle the clay herself, and the teacher talked with her about what was happening. Jerome Bruner has found that mental images of reality change most readily when there is active physical involvement (enactive), plus verbal reflection including what he calls "labeling." In labeling the teacher may point out significant facts. ("Where did the extra clay go?" "The pancake is wider but it is skinnier.") In an experiment, Bruner had one group of children watch the teacher manipulate the clay and then engage in the labeling process. A second group of children manipulated the clay, but there was no labeling. The third group both manipulated and participated in labeling. The children were all first graders who had been tested and had not been able to demonstrate an understanding of conservation of amount. As a result of this experiment, 40 percent of the children in the first group achieved conservation, 30 percent of the second group, and over 75 percent of the third group. This strongly points out the importance of both enactive and verbal activity in the development of new thinking structures.[7]

In the interviews with Janie, labeling and talking served the purpose of encouraging the rational, analytical, logical, verbal functions of Janie's mind. But the teacher was patient, aware that the construction of new mental images takes time. Janie was using the imaginative, creative powers of her mind in combination with the logical, when she came up with a new explanation—"I put it to itself, in the middle." Note that the teacher accepted this explanation. In fact, she was amazed and delighted. How much more exciting and original than a learned response! And how much more useful to the learner herself.

Most of us can probably find information ("Xs") floating around in our heads that does not connect with any meanings or experiences or realities in our lives. In my high school and college days, history stands out as an example of memorized dates, names, and places having no connection with anything significant to me. Consequently I disliked history, and it was not until years later that I discovered its relationship to people and meaning and how people make sense out of their world.

Today, children are learning basic skills and information to help them function in American society, but they are not using these skills to better their daily lives.

This is the major conclusion of a national study released . . . by the National Assessment of Educational Progress, a project of the Education Commission of the States. . . . Helen Masterson, a study-group official, says: "There has been great concern across the country about going back to the basics. From our studies, students have the basics in place, but when it goes to that next step of putting it all together to apply the skills they've learned to better their lives, they have problems. And we don't really know why this is."[8]

The study lists what children and youth at different ages can and cannot do. These lists suggest that much information has been successfully "poured into their heads," but that it was not used in conjunction with the developmental characteristics of the age groups. Thus, it has existed apart from the living meaning and experience of the individuals and may remain thus compartmentalized indefinitely.

Traditionally, learning has most often been understood as the transfer of information from one head, the teacher's, to other heads, the students' (see figure 1).

Developmental Journey

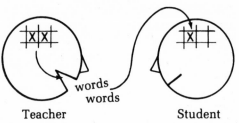

Teacher   Student

Figure 1

In this fourth response, I am describing another model in which the INSTRUCTOR (parent, teacher, or therapist) serves to facilitate the interaction of the STUDENT'S

—emotions
——rational-verbal-logical functions
———intuitive-imagistic-metaphorical functions
———physical activity (enactive)

with the SUBJECT MATTER, in the context of an accepting, supporting, challenging COMMUNITY. I call this model "confluent education," a term proposed by George Isaac Brown with a more restricted definition.[9] I use the term to mean the *flowing together of the functions of the whole person* in an encounter with the subject matter. This process is represented in the following diagram.

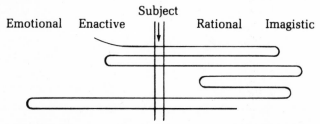

The flowing line indicates that the various functions can flow together. For instance, Janie started with an enactive operation—manipulating the clay balls. The questions asked of her engaged her thinking in both the

194

rational and imagistic modes. Her emotions became involved, although the interviewer did not raise the issue directly. The enactive operations continued throughout the session, often alternating with the rational and imagistic. Different sessions may stress different functions; the important point is that the instructor plan an overall balance for the students.

The approaches and activities described in the rest of the book presume their setting in a context of confluent learning.

STIMULATION OF DEVELOPMENT

Several factors have been shown to influence development defined as change in structure of thinking. These are:

1. exposure to conflicts in reasoning
2. exposure to the next higher stage of moral reasoning
3. role-taking opportunities
4. the operative level of justice of the environment

These factors have been tested to some extent in situations where pre- and post-testing of the individuals involved has been conducted in terms of stage of moral reasoning. Kohlberg and Blatt, for instance, report experiments in which there was a systematic attempt to stimulate the development of moral reasoning.[10] One program took place in a Jewish Reform school class of children ages eleven and twelve. There were three control groups, all of the same age, social class, and moral stages as the experimental group. The major finding was that the classroom experience of the experimental group led to a significant increase in moral judgment maturity and that the increase was still evident a year later. In contrast, none of the changes in the control groups was significant.

The materials used with the experimental group were a set of open-ended moral dilemmas which the children were asked to try to resolve. The children's suggestions were noted on the chalkboard, and the children were then asked to consider the consequences of each solution, for each of the characters in the dilemma. "In examining these consequences, the examiner attempted to point out psychological and social dimensions of the experiences involved. Next, children were asked to specify the standard or hierarchy of values implicit in each of the solutions."[11] Conflict was stimulated by the use of questions. All this was done in the context of attempting to establish an atmosphere of justice, in which there was freedom of expression and an understanding of different points of view, with effort made to clarify points of disagreement.

Such use of moral dilemmas has been the common practice in research designed to stimulate moral reasoning. The manner of presentation and the style of leadership apparently have some effect on the results. Results have not always been conclusive. Maureen Joy has written:

Long-term, not brief interventions, are required for an adequate program of moral education. . . . studies, such as the OISE Pickering study (Beck et al., 1972), indicate that a variety of experiences extended over at least a year produce significant results. The teacher's role is that of understanding students' level of development, encouraging through instruction, questioning, designing activities leading to a higher level of thinking.[12]

Kohlberg puts the rationale for development in terms of the social atmosphere, and recently, research has also moved in the direction of a broader approach to the stimulation of moral reasoning. Kohlberg describes two conditions of social atmosphere which, he says, stimulate the growth of moral reasoning. One of these conditions is the opportunity that is offered for role-taking, that is, encouraging the person to put him- or herself in the shoes of others or to take the point of view of others. The second condition is the level of justice of the environment or institution: "the justice structure of an institution refers to the perceived rules or principles for distributing rewards,

196

punishments, responsibilities, and privileges among institutional members."[13] As an example, a study of a traditional prison showed that inmates perceived it as Stage 1, regardless of their own stage of reasoning. They saw the institution as governed by power figures using arbitrary commands and dispensing punishment for the disobedient. In another prison, where a behavior modification approach gave point rewards for conformity to rules, the inmates saw the institution as a Stage 2 system of useful exchange. Inmates at Stages 3 and 4 saw this institution as more fair than the traditional one, but not really fair according to their own terms.

At the time of this writing, Kohlberg and associates are implementing a program to stimulate moral development in two high schools in the Boston area (Cambridge and Brookline) and two in Pittsburgh. The two dimensions of the program are:

1. the training of teachers and counselors to conduct and integrate moral discussions into the curriculum, and

2. the establishment of a "just community" or partici-patory democracy, with focus on real issues faced by the participants: drug use, stealing, disruptions, grading. One report of the beginning program at the Cambridge school said that a successful democratic community had been established in a just community composed of sixty-nine students and six teachers within the regular school. A sense of community and higher morale were the most immediate results. The report states:

Students have assumed increasing responsibility for their own behavior and for the behavior of others . . . friendships . . . have formed among students of widely different background. . . . The staff has observed some positive changes in the behavior of students with long histories of difficulty in school. . . . The staff believes that many students in the school have begun to progress in moral reasoning up the Kohlberg scale, but research to test this hypothesis has only begun.[14]

Additional programs to found schools based on develop-mental principles are in beginning stages.

I have been interested for some time in the effect that a thorough exposure to cognitive structural developmental theories might have on persons in their own development. We are starting to test for this variable in a current research project, and our first tentative results suggest that there is a stimulating effect.

Since cognitive structural developmental theory is based in an interactional model, requiring interaction between the individual's innate functioning and the environment, stimulation from the environment is necessary for development to occur. All that we have said so far in this section implies careful planning of the educational environment.

Since much of an individual's life is not spent in school, it is also important that we give attention to what goes on in the home and in other settings. Following the social perspective factor of community/society through the stages, we can see possible concerns appropriate for persons at different ages and stages. For instance, the young child needs to see the adults in his or her life as authorities if Stage 1 is to be achieved. In preparation for movement into Stage 2, fairness can be experienced in the family in a very concrete way through discussion and explanation of daily incidents. Children need to experience community and be encouraged to empathize in order to build toward Stage 3. Active participation in well-run institutional structures may enable development toward Stage 4. The enactive mode—physical participation—combined with reflection, analysis, and questioning could well be the key to maximum stimulation of development.

Once when I was pushing a class of new seventh-graders to think rather than to parrot right answers, a girl responded:

"But Mrs. Wilcox, I didn't know we were supposed to think." Perhaps this is a clue to what we are to be doing: enabling ourselves and others to participate and to *think* about our experience.

Before I move into descriptions of specific strategies, I am going to discuss briefly ethical distinctions in the challenging of children and youth and adults.

ETHICAL DISTINCTIONS:
CHILDREN, YOUTH, ADULTS

A major ethical concern of students of developmental theory centers on how much right the instructor has to challenge the thinking of the students, particularly if individuals evidence good coping abilities at their present stage. I think we need to look at this carefully and make distinctions between adults and other age groups.

CHILDREN

In most environments, children expect to receive and to develop new ideas, new ways of looking at the world. Change is a way of life, both physically and intellectually. Perhaps the major problem encountered is when such change is not facilitated, for instance, if the child's normal curiosity is stifled. Children generally enjoy the growing that results from stimulation of their reasoning.

As I have stated earlier, I consider it unethical to allow children to remain unchallenged and unstimulated. I consider it the responsibility of parents, schools, and society to foster such stimulation that children may get a good start on the journey toward their ultimate potential.

YOUTH

In general the same factors pertain to the education of youth. One high school student wrote this paragraph in response to an invitation to students to comment on schools and education.

I've sat through dozens of boring lectures and it always makes me wonder whether maybe I'll wake up some morning and find myself ensconced in apathy with all my ideas and ideals vanished. Teachers of America, you are not being paid to babysit but to stimulate. If that's too demanding, don't tamper with my life anymore.[15]

199

I believe we have an ethical responsibility to challenge in general. In addition, since we live in a democratic society, we have the responsibility to enable high school graduates to live as responsible citizens in a democratic society. The pervasive relativism infecting our culture today does not seem to be good preparation for principled decision-making. Stimulation toward a Stage 4 perspective may well be a concrete objective for high schools. A Stage 5 social perspective and moral reasoning seem highly desirable for responsible decision-making in a democratic society, and development toward Stage 4 in high school might make this a possibility for more citizens.

But sensitivity toward and respect for each individual must not be sacrificed in the interests of overall goals, no matter how worthy they may appear to be.

ADULTS

Working with adults involves the simultaneous balancing of individual needs and desires and the stimulation of a shaping vision in the individual. Many adults have consolidated previous learnings into structures that are comfortable and appear to serve them well. They do not experience growth and change to any significant extent and may see change as threatening rather than desirable. Many do not know that change is possible. Others may be in the midst of painful transition and require direction and support in order to achieve new equilibrium. And some welcome challenges and change and alternatives.

Balancing respect for the integrity of adults and their value commitments, that may involve strong emotional ties, with their potential for growth and their needs to consolidate transitional structures, means that working with adults requires special sensitivity. Adults have the same right to be given the opportunity to grow, and they also have the right to continue in the use of present structures without undue pressures to change.

At any age there is the need to sharpen the use of present structures on different content, and this approach may be particularly appropriate as a major goal for adult study. Familiar contemporary social problems present a variety of issues that can be discussed by adults with real learning when the decision-making situations are handled in a constructive way. The decision-making and educational models I have described in previous chapters provide structures for approaching controversial problems.

Strategies described in the next chapter suggest ways in which adults can develop more complexity within their present stage. Role-taking, for instance, may help one to see other points of view and may encourage increased use of "B" modes (meaning that the stage of reasoning is becoming more inclusive, reversible, and balanced) rather than "A" modes in a particular stage.

New content may be added for the purpose of enlarging adults' views or meaning structure of reality, thus revealing previously unknown facets of familiar situations. In this process stereotypes may be changed, perhaps in the direction of a greater correspondence to a shaping vision.

Where careful attention is paid to the dynamics of a learning situation, where leader and group members become sensitive to one another and can challenge or support as needed, each individual can be free to respond in his or her own way. Experiences involving the whole person within the context of a supportive community provide the setting for maximum achievement and satisfaction for most persons.[16]

Hi Dad
I wonder if you'll ever
read this book again
I hope so because
then you'll know that
I really value
Friendship
an awful
lot.
Ma..
2..

Case studies as defined
need to be further
separation no their
using justice issues to
incl.

QUIZ

Match the statements in Column A with the answers in Column B.

Column A	Column B
1. If there is no such thing as "value-free education," we need to be aware of _____	1. moral dilemmas and participatory democracy (the "just community").
2. Vices and virtues are necessary parts of moral development but should not be used to _____	2. what values are being taught.
3. Relativism may be a different kind of _____	3. absolutism.
4. Developmental theory tells us that subject matter will be interpreted _____	4. define its ends.
5. Two approaches to stimulating development used in research settings have been _____	5. threatening and undesirable.
6. Children and youth expect change; some adults may see change as _____	6. in different ways at different stages.

ANSWERS
1. 2   2. 4   3. 3   4. 6   5. 1   6. 5

CHAPTER XI
So What Do I Do Now?

"So what do I do now with all this theory? How can I put it to use?"

This is the question most commonly asked by students as they approach the end of a course in cognitive development. From a research point of view we do not have much conclusive data showing what is effective and what is not. But people have been trying different things, have reported exciting experiences, and it is from this information that I have drawn the descriptions that follow.

Sarah, mother of three adolescents, was a student in one of my graduate school classes. One day during the third week of the course she came in early, excited and wanting to talk about an experience that week. She related a dinner table conversation in which her adolescent daughter had broached a subject that usually provoked conflict and hard feelings. On this last occasion Sarah had kept quiet, had listened, and then had asked "why" questions. All the while she had made a conscious effort to get inside the world-view of her daughter in contrast to previous occasions when she had felt threatened, angry, and judgmental.

When Sarah came to class she was feeling good about herself, about her daughter, and about the beginning communication that had taken place. She said that she thought she had learned something about role-taking. And she had discovered that *reasons*, the answers to "why" questions, are often more important for understanding than the conclusions which are usually stated first (and often attacked). Sarah's relationship with her children continued to change throughout the time period of the course, changed in the direction of better communication and better feelings on both sides.

Pat, another student, wrote about a new understanding she had of her experience in interviewing and scoring another adult:

This interview was an important learning experience for me because I know the person to be a well-educated individual who takes a responsible role in the community, shows active concern for others, and has been exposed to a short course in cognitive development. By my scoring she is solidly in Stage 3. Throughout much of the class I have been concerned with the general attitude that any stage short of 5 was to be looked down on as inadequate, and I must admit that in the past I have been guilty of this attitude myself. Now I see that persons can function adequately in whatever stage they have reached.

Sarah and Pat have each changed in themselves and in the way they relate to other persons, and the changes have been very satisfying to them. Perhaps this is where we need to start—with ourselves—asking the questions: How do I perceive other people? Can I put myself in their shoes? If we begin to struggle with these questions, as did Sarah and Pat, then perhaps we are ready to explore how we can use developmental theory to serve others.

COMMUNICATION

Sarah has given us an example of how developmental theory can inform our understandings in communication and our acceptance of other persons and their ideas. The implications of developmental theory can be carried into any situation—home, work, school, volunteer activities. In the following incident, we see how this approach to communication is also utilized to encourage moral reasoning and decision-making.

Janie, 5, and Carlie, 4, had come to visit grandma for the weekend. Grandma gave each of the little girls ten pennies. Later she noticed that Janie had 14 pennies and Carlie had six. Janie insisted that she had not taken any from Carlie, that she had brought them with her in her purse. (She did bring a purse containing an unknown number of pennies.) What should the grandmother do and say?

I have used this story a number of times with groups of parents and teachers. A common response is that the grandmother should insist that Janie return the pennies, that she should not be allowed to get away with such behavior.

I give these directions for thinking about the dilemma in a different way.

How might the grandmother deal with this situation in terms of Stages 1 and 2 social perspective and moral reasoning? Her purpose would be to help Janie to reason morally rather than to return the pennies, since there is room for doubt about Janie's culpability.

Here is what actually happened when the grandmother used this second approach. (It might be helpful to refer to the foldout at end of this book.) She told Janie that she had wanted Janie and Carlie to each have ten pennies and that she didn't like it that Janie now had more. (Note the use of Stage 1 social perspective related to what "the big person" wanted. Punishment was purposely not mentioned, however, in order to avoid accusing Janie in case she was innocent.) The grandmother then asked Janie how she would feel if Carlie had more pennies (encouraging some role-taking) and pointed out that it wasn't fair for Janie to have more than Carlie (using some simple Stage 2 reasoning). Janie did not want to comment, and the subject was dropped. An hour or so later the grandmother noted that Janie and Carlie each had ten pennies.

This case, in which Carlie was unaware that she was on the short end of the deal, and there was no way of proving wrongdoing (Carlie might well have lost the pennies), provided an ideal situation for Janie to be encouraged to do some moral reasoning. Unfortunately we do not know what went on in her mind since she declined to discuss the subject! But we do know that she was not accused—possibly unjustly; that she was not treated as a potential delinquent; and that she was presented with appropriate "thinking" tools for making a moral decision.

I am not suggesting that every situation with a five-year-old is a suitable one for stimulating moral decision-making. When one child is beating another over the head with a toy metal truck, one does not calmly say, "Let us reason together." Or if Janie had reacted with great emotional distress, it might have been unwise to push her to make a decision. The adult needs to try to provide a supportive community.

This incident is an example of two ways of using developmental theory. First, it suggests possibilities for communicating with others and for stimulating moral reasoning. It is impossible to anticipate one's own response to such incidents when they arise, but one can be alert to them in a different way and be prepared for different options in handling them. A first step is to learn to listen and ask the "why" questions—Why do you think that? Why did you come to that conclusion?—and then respect the answers.

Second, stories such as this may form the basis for classes to try some straight role-playing or to practice using social perspective and moral reasoning at Stages 1 and 2, as suggested by the portions in italics.

Here are two more incidents drawn from real life that I have used to help students practice the use of developmental theory.

Fifth-grader Anne came home from school with an expensive ball point pen which she had bought from a friend for 25 cents. The friend had several such pens she was selling. Anne admitted to her parents that her friend might have stolen the pens, but she stubbornly refused to return the pen and would under no circumstances consider that either she or her parents report the theft to the teacher or principal. That would be betraying her friend.

In terms of Stages 2 and 3 moral reasoning, how might the

parents deal with this incident to help Anne reason morally about it?

This is not an easy situation to respond to in terms of most adult concepts of behavior because of the strong dyadic perspective characteristic of both Stage 2 and 3.

Here is another true story:

Several incidents have taken place at the youth center. There is good reason to believe that members of the junior high group were involved. The incidents involved:

1-throwing snowballs at passing cars (*blinding drivers*).

2-using permanent felt-tip markers to write obscene words on the walls of one of the rooms. (*Volunteer workers had to repaint the room.*)

3-breaking toys and furniture in a room used as a weekday nursery for less-privileged preschool children.

Concentrating on Stages 2 and 3, how would you as an adult leader of junior-highs deal with this situation in order to get the junior highs to reason morally about it?

In the actual situation, the junior highs were asked to rank these incidents from worst to least reprehensible. The consequences, in italics above, were not included in their lists. The young persons were then asked to share their rankings and to give reasons for them. It was interesting that the junior highs did not generate any consequences for the first and second incidents, but several expressed moral concern that "Those little children wouldn't have things to play with." They also thought that writing obscene words on the walls of a room where younger children were was bad, but were not particularly concerned with the act itself. The responsibility of adult leaders became that of describing other consequences and helping the junior highs to understand the roles of the blinded drivers and volunteer painters.

Such stories not only provide good classroom material for adults, but also make good discussion starters for family conversations, opening up opportunities for communication and stimulation of moral reasoning.

Again, it is important to keep in mind such guidelines as: listen, accept, ask for reasons, try not to get uptight!

MORAL DILEMMAS

The moral dilemma, often mentioned in this book, is the vehicle most commonly used by Kohlberg for the stimulation of moral reasoning. He predicates its use on the basis of three characteristics of moral development which I will repeat here:

1. Most persons can understand reasoning about moral issues at the next higher stage above their major stage, but no higher.

2. Individuals generally prefer reasoning at the highest stage they can understand.

3. When persons are exposed to reasoning about moral issues one stage above theirs, especially through repeated exposures, they tend to move to that next higher stage.

Discussion of moral issues creates the situation in which such growth becomes possible. However, the use of moral dilemmas also has objectives broader than those of stimulating moral reasoning. Barry K. Beyer has suggested five such goals:

1. Improving learning skills—listening, oral communication, the ability to participate constructively in group discussions.

2. Improving self-esteem—treating each other's ideas with respect.

3. Improving attitudes toward school—moral discussions are usually perceived as interesting and relevant.

4. Improving knowledge of key concepts—for instance, justice.

5. Facilitating stage change.

"As a result of several years of moral discussions as an integral part of social studies classes, the typical high school student who began as a freshman thinking in a mixture of Stage 2 and 3 terms will think predominately at Stage 4."[1]

Moral dilemmas can be derived from actual situations or from available materials.[2] They should be simple problem situations which allow for a variety of answers and in which moral issues come into conflict. The dilemma and the questions which follow its presentation must be open-ended in order to allow a full range of reasoning rather than to provide any structures which would lead toward predetermined conclusions. In light of this, the use of questions which elicit "should" reasons rather than "would" behaviors is of critical importance. In the Heinz dilemma, moral reasoning requires consideration of what Heinz *should* do rather than all the things that students think they *would* do. The task is to solve the moral dilemma, not to explore all the alternative ways that Heinz might get the money (as did Janie's first answers to the dilemma in chapter 4). In a classroom discussion it is often necessary for the teacher to help class members focus on the moral issues, the "shoulds," and not on alternative actions that leave the site of conflicting issues.

Beyer lists five sequential activities for class members in order to facilitate effective moral discussions.[3]

1. Confront a dilemma
2. Recommend tentative courses of action to resolve the dilemma and justify these recommendations
3. Discuss reasons in small groups
4. Examine the reasoning of the class as they justify recommended solutions to the dilemma
5. Reflect on their reasoning as they bring temporary closure to the discussion

There are other activities that vary the way moral dilemmas are used and which may promote participation, understanding, and role-taking. Some dilemmas are available in filmstrips and movies, or they can be dramatized by group members.

Solutions to a dilemma can be role-played by different students, or individuals can write or draw endings for the story. Teams can be formed to debate two conflicting solutions, but may have to be reminded to give *reasons* to justify their conclusions.

To open the discussion of a dilemma, I have sometimes started with values voting or a values continuum, described more fully in the section on values-clarification. For instance, after telling the Heinz dilemma, I might ask: How many of you think that Heinz should steal the drug? (values voting). Or I will set up two ends of a continuum —Heinz absolutely should steal the drug versus Heinz absolutely should not steal the drug—and then ask people to stand on the line between the two extremes according to their own position on the issue. In both cases the activity is followed by a discussion of reasons.

As suggested in the last section, moral dilemmas and other such activities can be used at home as well as in school and church. They may also be used to introduce issues requiring decisions by committees. Whether in class or elsewhere, it is necessary to remember that we are looking for reasons for moral decisions, that all reasons must be accepted, and that in most settings participants reason from more than one stage. This creates a natural situation in which group members can hear reasons from stages other than their own. It is not necessary for the leader to be an expert at identifying such stages (a risky business at best!); however, the following age groupings are helpful to keep in mind when planning:

Preschool: stages 0 and 1.
Elementary school: stages 1 and 2, some 0 and some 3.
Junior high: stages 2 and 3, some 1.
Senior high: stages 2 and 3, some 1 and some 4.
Adults: stages 3 and 4, some 1, 2, and 5.

VALUES-CLARIFICATION

Values-clarification has been mentioned several times in this book. It is an approach that was made popular several years ago with the publication of the book, *Values Clarification*, and that book has been followed by a number of others. The aim of values-clarification is stated thus:

> . . . the values-clarification approach does not aim to instill any particular set of values. Rather the goal of the values-clarification approach is to help students utilize the . . . processes of valuing in their own lives; to apply these valuing processes to already formed beliefs and behavior patterns and to those still emerging.[4]

I have previously raised questions about the use and misuse of values-clarification strategies. My purpose in this section is to give examples of how such strategies can be used constructively within the context of the educational model I have proposed, and specifically how they relate to the stimulation of moral reasoning.

It may be helpful to distinguish between the kinds of values or moral issues that Kohlberg defines, and the more general choices and preferences included in the values-clarification approach. Kohlberg is concerned with moral judgments of right and wrong in situations where moral values come into conflict. Values-clarification covers the field of general values such as, how one likes to spend time and money, what one does or does not like about oneself, what one *would* do in certain situations. It does include moral issues, but does not center on them, nor is it concerned with reasons. Both general values and moral values are of great importance, and clarification of general values often raises questions of moral values. I make regular use of values-clarification strategies and find their description in different publications very helpful. However, I first decide what my purpose is and then select those strategies that lead toward that purpose. I propose the following guidelines for such selection.

1. Define the specific issues or concerns with which the students will be involved.

2. Select strategies that help to clarify those concerns and any conflicts among them.

3. Select strategies that encourage free expression of

opinions, thoughts, and feelings and that encourage participants to take the role of others. Values-clarification strategies are very helpful here.

4. Concentrate on reasons for answers, not just the decisions themselves. This approach is not inherent in values-clarification strategies, and must be built into the learning process. Neither is values-clarification concerned with providing reasons one stage above the highest level used by the students, although this may be a byproduct of the open discussion encouraged by values-clarification.

With these guidelines in mind, next I will describe some examples that I have used in the educational context of the model I have proposed.

WHERE DO YOU STAND? (VALUES CONTINUUM)

The purpose of this strategy is to help persons be aware of their own thinking about the law, to provide opportunity for exchange of views, to hear one another's reasons, to stimulate conflict in reasoning, and to increase ability to take the role of other persons.[5]

Directions: Make two separate signs on large paper, one saying "Lawful Larry: Always Obeys All Laws" and the other saying "Do-Your-Own-Thing Donna: Disregards Laws with Which She Disagrees." (Supply names of your choice in order to avoid embarrassment to group members. Also, descriptions of Lawful Larry and Donna can be given orally in order to avoid large, complicated signs.) Place the two signs on the floor or wall with sufficient space between them so that all participants can sit or stand in the space. Explain that we are going to set up a continuum and that the statements represent two extremes. Each person is to decide where he or she stands—with Lawful Larry, with Donna, or somewhere in between. After each person, including teachers or leaders, has taken a position, discuss reasons for the choices. No person should be forced to participate. Allow changing of positions. If students cluster near Donna, giving what sound like Stage 2 and 3 reasons (a common response), a teacher or leader might take a position in sympathy with Lawful Larry and try some Stage 4 reasoning.

This strategy can be extended by introducing a moral dilemma, for instance, describing a situation involving illegal use of drugs or mercy-killing or illegal governmental activities, and again asking each participant to take a position on the continuum. In each case, discuss choices with emphasis on the reasons for them. Such activities can be used to introduce units of study, thus combining moral reasoning with a personalized interest in the subject matter.

Such a continuum may also be used to help students of almost any age express reactions to a class. Using the signs, "Confused Confucius" and "Clear-as-a-Bell Clarinda," students position themselves on the continuum according to how they are feeling about the course and then explain their reasons. This does not, of course, involve moral reasoning, but is a very useful activity for the teacher who is seriously interested in feedback and clarification of student problems.

VALUES VOTING

This is another strategy I use frequently to stimulate reasoning and free discussion.[6] In values voting, participants are asked a question and then indicate their votes by:
- —hand raised to signify a yes vote
- —hand raised and waved to signify an enthusiastic yes vote
- —thumb down to signify a no vote
- —thumb down with agitated movement to signify an enthusiastic no vote
- —arms folded to signify undecided
- —sit as is to indicate no participation

This is a good opener for a new group because participants usually find it fun and nonthreatening. We

213

may start a new course in cognitive development by asking a values voting question: How many of you think it is all right to break the law? After the group members have given their reasons for their answers, we lead them to reflect on similarities and differences, and to distinguish between conclusions and reasons. People may come to opposite conclusions for similar reasons, or may agree in their conclusions but use very different reasons. It is important to help participants be aware of this as such an awareness prepares them for a subsequent look at content and structure of moral reasoning.

RANK ORDERS

Rank orders is another strategy helpful in stimulating conflict in reasoning, exchanging points of view, and becoming aware of one's priorities.[7] The following variation which I developed for use with elementary school children has also been useful with youth and adults because its concreteness helps persons to focus.

Directions: Give each student a prepared set of five or six cards or slips of paper, each card printed with a behavior description. Such behaviors might include:

—telling a lie
—making somebody else
  feel badly
—disobeying a rule
  or a law
—disobeying parents
  or teacher
—disobeying your own
  conscience
—breaking a promise

Instruct everyone to choose the card that he or she thinks describes the worst behavior of those listed. Stick it near the top of a strip of masking tape, leaving about an inch of free tape at the top. Then choose the card that represents the best or "least worst" thing you might do. Put it at the bottom of the tape. Next arrange the other cards on the tape in order from "worst" to "least worst!" The top of the tape can then be attached to a table edge, the back of a chair, or a bulletin board while the participants discuss the reasons for their choices. They should be encouraged to rearrange their cards if they change their minds during the discussion.

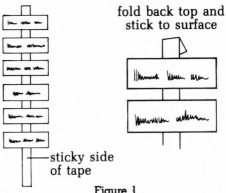

fold back top and
stick to surface

sticky side
of tape

Figure 1

The behaviors selected for the cards should relate to the stages of moral reasoning of the age group. Those I have suggested make sense to elementary school children, youth, and adults, although usually for different reasons. For instance, "disobeying parents or teacher" might be a "worst thing" for a child in terms of punishment; for an adult it might be seen in terms of lack of respect.

RULE-MAKING

Rule-making is an activity which can be used in home, church, or school to help individuals experience how rules and laws allow a community to function in an orderly manner. It is a facet, and an important one, of the "just community." It is particularly appropriate for older elementary school children and youth and can occur at the beginning of a program year, before an outing, or as the result of some incident requiring reflection and evaluation. One alternative to rule-making is the imposition of rules on a group, rules that have been formulated by an institution and for which reasons are not clear. Another alternative is to simply hope that the group will not do anything that will cause trouble or embarrass the sponsoring institution. In terms of developmental theory, rule-making seems to be the most appropriate response.

(It also produces consistently better results in terms of behavior!)

Instructions. As an example let's say a group of youth is meeting to plan a field trip. Along with other practical concerns, raise the question of what might happen that could spoil the trip for everyone (individuals getting lost or hurt, illegal use of drugs and alcohol, etc.). What would be some of the consequences of these? (Danger, worried leaders, parents, or students, legal difficulties, blame on leaders, etc.) It is important to remember that some youth are not able to generate logical consequences to behavior, so leaders may have to help with this by raising some of the questions.

The next step is to look at some alternative solutions for avoiding problems and plan how these might be implemented.

Each of these steps can be accomplished through brain-storming examples of specific problems that have arisen on previous occasions, and through role-taking activities. In a democratic atmosphere students and leaders alike can feel free to offer ideas. The leaders may have to explain the concern and regulations of the institution involved (school, family, camp, church) since institutions have built-in responsibilities and expectations that need to be considered.

With this kind of a setting youth can begin to understand rules and institutional procedures as positive forces intended for the good of all rather than as commands from self-serving authoritative persons.

ROLE-PLAY

I have been using the term "role-taking" to mean our basic orientation toward other people in relation to how we imagine ourselves in their places or how we walk in the shoes of another. The term "role-playing" refers to a *specific activity* in which people *practice* putting themselves in the situations of others. One of its major purposes is to stimulate the development of role-taking ability. A role-play can range from a guided dramatic activity, in which a story is acted out in informal fashion, to complex simulation games.

In true role-playing there is little structure, and this makes it difficult to use with children under the age of nine or ten, especially since their cognitive development limits their role-taking ability. Informal but guided dramatization of stories is suitable for these younger children.

A role-play involves assigning a role to each partici-pant, then describing a situation and asking the role-play-ers to play out the part as they think it would or should be done in those circumstances. One example of a role-play is given in an exercise at the end of chapter 7. In the next chapter, I have given complete directions for a role-play that helps older youth and adults "get inside" the Stage 4 structure exemplified by the Pharisees.

Role-playing needs to be used with care as it can tap strong emotions. Some people are very self-conscious about participating in such activities, and no one should ever be pressured to do so. Persons may be encouraged to participate in very small groups, within a climate of acceptance and opportunity to try new things. Role-play-ers should be discouraged from overplaying or "hamming up" a role. This distorts the characters as well as the meanings that might be derived from the experience. The audience should refrain from comments and excessive laughter. Debriefing of the experience is essential, and usually starts by offering the role-players opportunity to express how they felt. After feelings have been expressed, role-players and audience can further pursue meanings and implications.

A DEVELOPMENTAL INTERPRETATION GRID

A developmental interpretation grid is a basic and simple scheme to help the instructor organize subject matter according to the developmental levels of students. It points out where students may have difficulty in appropriating concepts and warns the instructor of potential problems.

To demonstrate the use of the grid, I have at hand a lesson on justice intended for eighth graders. After carefully studying it myself, I made a list of the major concepts that are emphasized. These are:

1. universal justice for all people
2. community as represented by political institutions
3. individual responsibility through political action

These are abbreviated and written into the headings of the columns under "Concepts, Issues, Symbols, Images, Etc."

DEVELOPMENTAL INTERPRETATION GRID

MODEL/ THEORY	STAGE/ LEVEL PERIOD	CONCEPTS, ISSUES, SYMBOLS, IMAGES, ETC.		
		Universal Justice	Individual responsibility	Community, political institutions

Developmental theory informs me that eighth graders are probably a mixture of Stage 2 and 3 social perspective and moral reasoning and may range from concrete operational to various levels of formal operations. How can this information help me plan the lesson so that the subject matter might have some real meaning for the students?

My first step is to look at the various models in order to explore which ones may be most informative on the subject of justice. Kohlberg's moral reasoning material describes conceptions of justice at different stages. Again abbreviating, I enter "Moral Reasoning" and "Justice" in the left-hand column, and "Stage 2" and "Stage 3" in the next column. I then enter descriptions of Justice for Stage 2 and Stage 3 in the column headed "universal justice."

| MODEL/ THEORY | STAGE/ LEVEL PERIOD | CONCEPTS, ISSUES, SYMBOLS, IMAGES, ETC. | | |
		Universal Justice	Individual responsibility	Community, political institutions
Moral Reasoning	Stage 2	most "useful" people have priority		
Justice	Stage 3	"good" people and less fortunate people have priority		

The social perspective model offers insight into two other areas: community/society and role-taking, related to the other concepts in the lesson. This information is noted in the last two columns:

Social Perspective Community, society	Stage 2			Dyadic. Function of gov't is to prevent concrete destructive behavior.
	Stage 3			Dyadic empathetic. Small groups are the structure of society. Benevolent leadership promotes good as defined by one's group.
Role-taking	Stage 2		Limited ability to relate to the situation of others	
	Stage 3		Empathy for less fortunate people	

For this particular lesson we could look at other models such as that of Erik H. Erikson.[8] We also need to consider the practical realities in which junior-highs find themselves. For instance, what can an eighth-grader do in society?

The information on the chart suggests that the concept of universal justice is one of those shaping visions that is not automatically relevant to persons at Stages 2 and 3, and that the concept of working through political systems is conceptually and practically unrealistic for junior-highs.

My approach to teaching this material, which I did in a demonstration workshop where I did not know the young people, was first of all to involve them on a personal level in the subject matter. I posted pictures illustrating situations of human need in which justice might be applied. I asked the students to move around the room and look at the pictures, choosing one or two that depicted something that they personally were concerned about.

In the discussion that followed, there was enthusiastic agreement with a suggestion by one student that helping people should begin at home, that we should not have to worry about "all those people far away." The expressed views of the vocal students were consistent with a Stage 3 social perspective, as predicted. Two major questions need to be considered in follow-up sessions on this unit:

1. What strategies can be used to confront these students with a shaping vision of universal justice that will challenge their present content?

2. How can a community of support enable them to act responsibly in terms of engaging their present concerns as well as the vision of universal justice? Engaging social perspectives at Stages 2 and 3 would imply focusing on dyadic relationships, and, in order to move toward the shaping vision, such relationships might include individuals in institutional structures to whom junior-highs are realistically related.

It has been my experience that use of the developmental interpretation grid not only raises relevant questions related to the students' probable grasp of material, but also opens up new vistas for the instructor. Accepted assumptions may be challenged, facilitating new awareness in role-taking. As I explored a particular concept in this way, it suddenly became clear to me why other people had different perceptions of it than I did. Use of the developmental interpretation grid is not restricted to instructors. It has been used by parents to clarify family issues and by pastors in preparing sermons. It enables one to explore a subject from different points of view and take the roles of other persons. I will give some other examples of its use in the chapter that follows.

ASKING QUESTIONS

Questions can be a nuisance when the three-year-old keeps up a running sequence of why? why? why? They can be embarrassing and uncomfortable when one is called on in class and cannot think of an answer. They can elicit information when we need it, and this is usually thought to be their main purpose. Yet in one book the title of the first chapter is "Questions Designed for More Than Memory."[9] The author, Norris M. Sanders, describes seven categories of questions of which only the first is concerned with eliciting facts and emphasizing memory. Although we do not usually think of using questions as stimulators of thought, Sanders' six remaining categories describe ways of stimulating six other kinds of thinking. However, it is stressed that the seven categories of questions are sequential and cumulative, that is, each builds on the previous categories or levels.

These seven categories relate directly to developmental theory and are very important in a developmental approach to education. The first four categories can be used in concrete operational thinking and, with limitations, by those at preoperational levels. The last three require formal operations, yet can be used as a shaping vision for less complex levels.

As I write these last sentences I am aware once again of my own frustration at the self-imposed limitations in writing this book. I would like to explore at length the relationships between developmental theory and the asking of questions. But instead I can only summarize, offer other resources, and encourage the interested reader to pursue the subject.

221

In my own summary form, here are the seven levels of questions proposed by Sanders.

1. Memory/fact: recognition and/or recall of information.
2. Translation: changing information into a different symbolic form or different words. (draw a picture, dramatize, write a paraphrase)
3. Interpretation/comparison: perceiving relationships, implications, cause and effect, and analogy on the commonsense level. Information used as instructed. Classification. (compare, contrast, relate)
4. Application: transfer of meaning to a new situation, moving outside of instruction. Deals with the whole of ideas and skills, not just the parts.

When using levels of questioning based on 1 through 4 above, thought *content* will be stimulated to reach conclusions based on commonsense without consciousness of the thought processes involved. Levels 2 through 4 are based on the premise that accurate information has been obtained at the first level (memory/fact) of questioning. The following levels—5 through 7—require formal operations.

5. Analysis: requires problem-solving in light of *conscious* knowledge of the parts and forms of thinking.
6. Synthesis: combining of past experiences to create an original product. Imagination, original thinking. Requires knowledge, competency in subject matter, divergent thinking, consideration of many possible answers.
7. Evaluation: not personal whim. Related to comparison but requires two steps: setting of standards and determining how closely an idea or object meets those standards.

We need to take seriously the sequential nature of questions because starting with questions of analysis, for instance, would short-circuit the process. How can a person analyze until he or she has the facts of the situation in mind? A good rule of thumb is to begin with questions of fact before moving into the process of stimulating cognitive reasoning. Play around with questions at the first four levels. Then, with youth and adult groups, try questions at levels 5, 6, and 7. This sequence can accomplish several goals:

1. It treats the subject matter with respect, allowing students to get a grasp of content before trying to use it or evaluate it.

2. It enables students to come together at the concrete level where there can be common understanding of the facts.

3. It enables each student to feel that he or she has some understanding of the subject matter, which can be very affirming.

4. Use of higher level questions in sequence may stimulate movement from concrete to formal operations for some students and stimulates interest and reasoning for students who are already formal operational.

SUMMARY

The intent of this chapter has been to open up possibilities for the application of cognitive developmental theory and to describe some concrete examples of how the theory is being used. It is hoped that the reader will make use of the bibliography to find further resources, thus approaching the challenges with creativity and industry, and contributing to a growing field.

Note that there is no quiz at the end of this chapter. Why not try a developmental interpretation grid for some subject that interests you?

CHAPTER XII
The Faith Dimension

INTRODUCTION

Developmental journey as I have described it is a lifelong process of trying to make sense out of, and finding meaning in, our total environment. This environment includes things, people, and moral issues: the objects of our logical thinking, our social perspective, and our moral reasoning. It also includes ways in which we try to put all this together. James Fowler describes this as a "way of knowing, of construing, or of interpreting experience . . . one's sense of relatedness to the ultimate conditions and depths of existence." Fowler calls this "faith development," and he says that faith understood in this way is not necessarily *synonomous* with any particular religion, tradition, or set of beliefs. However, it may include any of these as content.[1]

I like Fowler's definition and consider it wholly compatible with the thrust of this book. All aspects of the developmental journey can be seen as structure filled in by varying kinds of content. In this chapter I will be drawing upon my own content, my own experiences and research related to the Christian tradition, in order to include *practical* material for the use of cognitive developmental theory in a religious setting. I hope that persons who do not share this particular heritage will be able to translate the ideas and suggestions for use within their own traditions, whether sacred or secular.

In this chapter I explore five areas: Interpretation, Practical Activities, Reaching People, Misuses, and The Shaping Vision, with the basic understandings drawn from our own research.[2]

The goal of our 1975 research project was to examine

possible relationships between a person's stage of moral reasoning and his or her interpretation of a biblical text. Our subjects were children, youth, and adults with a wide diversity of religious backgrounds, ranging from a token year in Sunday school to professional training for the ministry. Each person was scored on the Heinz dilemma and was asked questions about a biblical text, Matthew 12:9-14 (see Appendix B). In both the dilemma and the text the issues of law and life are pivotal which provided the opportunity to observe possible correlations. We found that the critical factor in interpretation was stage and not religious training or experience. Examples of that relationship between stage and interpretation are given in this next section.

INTERPRETATION

LAW

Law is an important theme throughout the Bible, and Matthew 12:9-14 illustrates an attitude of Jesus toward the law. We asked the question, *Should Jesus have broken the law?* The major stage of the person responding is shown in the chart below.

Stage of Moral Reasoning	Replies
Stage 1	It's all right 'cause Jesus is the boss.
Stage 2	Yes, I think it is a good thing to do at least one or two good deeds on Sunday.
Stage 3	Yes, because he was totally giving. Yeah, because he was helping somebody.
Stage 4	Yes, but the question might be raised, could not Jesus have waited until Monday? If it was a matter of life and death, yes, in certain conditions. It's a question of priorities.

Stage 5	It's a question of how the law is interpreted. Jesus was not intending to do away with the law . . . It bothers me in terms of the effect it's going to have on the Pharisees if they see the law as keeping their whole religious system from falling apart. Maybe Jesus is trying to change the law, to allow them to treat people with mercy.

Note some of the stage characteristics: the authority figure at Stage 1, the bookkeeper at Stage 2, and the importance of good intentions at Stage 3. It is not until Stage 4 moral reasoning is used by individuals that they perceive the tension between the law and the actions of Jesus. This is also a major point of the text. At lower Stages (1 through 3) breaking the law is sanctioned without question on the basis of individualistic authority and/or good intentions. This text can reinforce Stage 2 and 3 relativistic world-views in which breaking the law is a personal decision based on individual needs or good intentions. Being aware of the actual meanings that are constructed by an intended audience raises serious questions about how we choose biblical material for teaching.

ROLE-TAKING

I have previously quoted replies to the question: *From the standpoint of society, were the Pharisees justified in being upset with Jesus?* Here are additional quotations from other stages.

Stage of Moral Reasoning	Replies
Stage 1	They're bad, they're going to kill Jesus.
Stage 2	No, they wanted to be the big cheese, see that people obeyed the law.

Stage 3   No, I wouldn't be upset if someone was breaking the law in that way.

Well, you know their interpretation. The Bible thing happened so long ago, is so irrelevant, that type of breaking the law seems to have been disproved as the Pharisees were all wrong to begin with.

Stage 4   Well, yeah, they had to answer to their society. You've got to understand that they have their own standards, and I suppose by their standards you just flat should not break the law.

Yeah, in their understanding they wanted to be a righteous people. They had a right to be angry.

Yes, because he posed a very definite threat to the stability of society.

Stage 5   I think they were very justified. If they see laws as concrete and needing to be obeyed to keep their whole religious system from falling apart. . . .

As I have just described, it is not until there is Stage 4 reasoning that a person is able to take the role of the Pharisees and perceive the source of conflict from their point of view. Probably the best known mandate for role-taking is the Golden Rule: "Do for others what you want them to do for you."[3] One assumption is that this means we each would want *someone else* to understand *our* point of view, rather than simply assume that ours is the same as theirs. At Stages 1, 2, and 3 the replies show no awareness that the Pharisees were perceiving the situation from a radically different point of view. I think the same would hold true in a contemporary situation. At Stages 1, 2, and 3 one would be unable to take the role of another person who was responding from a Stage 4 perspective. Such data is very challenging if we are concerned with the appropriation of such basic concepts as the Golden Rule and the related, "Love your neighbor as yourself." The stimulation of role-taking might be an important goal for religious education.

SYMBOLS

Throughout the stage descriptions earlier in the book I have given short examples of Fowler's aspect of symbol. In his available writings, Fowler has not defined what he means by the term "symbol." In our teaching of developmental theory, we find it helpful to describe five kinds of symbols.[4]

1. Symbolic names and people—God, Jesus, Abraham Lincoln

2. Symbolic objects—the cross, the communion cup, the flag

3. Symbolic statements—creeds and the "Pledge of Allegiance"

4. Symbolic acts (rituals)—a communion service, an Advent celebration, a graduation ceremony, standing to sing the national anthem

5. Symbolic stories (myths)—the Christmas story, the creation story, stories of George Washington, Abraham Lincoln, and the pilgrims

As we participate in symbols they consciously and subconsciously shape our beliefs and our lives. Symbols help us participate in the complex realities to which they refer. The influence may be either positive or negative. "God the father" may be a source of comfort to some persons, and a source of fear to others, depending on personal experiences. A worship service may produce awe, comfort, or boredom in different individuals.

Our first research project did not look for the meanings of symbols, but we accidentally found some. In chapter 2 Kathy used the symbol of God to explain why it would be bad to break the law: "God might see you and he can keep a-track of everybody . . . he can see everybody do everything."

Here we find an image of God that embodies the Stage 1 social perspective of the omnipotent authority. In

228

contrast, Hank, at Stage 2, presents an entirely different image of God in the following interview.

Interviewer: Is there anything unusual or special about church? Anything special about church?
Hank: You said if it was unusual.
I: Unusual?
H: That's what you said.
I: All right. Is there anything unusual about church for you?
H: No.
I: No? What does church mean to you?
H: It means God.
I: It means God?
H: And Jesus, and Mary, and the lamb, and the shepherds.
I: That's what it means?
H: Yes.
I: What does God mean to you? Who's God?
H: Who's God?
I: Yeah. What's God?
H: You know what's God.
I: Well, I have an idea of that. But what's your idea?
H: Love.
I: Love?
H: Love.
I: Love. What do you mean by that?
H: God—is—love. (Said very deliberately)
I: Yeah, but what does that mean to you?
H: It means loving each other, that's what it means.
I: Is that what it means? What does it mean to love each other?
H: I don't know what you're talking about.
I: Well, you just told me. You said, "God is love." and "Love means loving each other." and I just thought I'd ask you what you meant by that.
H: You know what I mean.
I: What would it mean for you to love Kathy?

229

H: I don't know what you mean.
I: How do you love Kathy?
H: I don't know what you're talking about.
I: Well, you just told me that God is love, right?
H: Right.
I: And that means loving somebody.
H: Yeah.
I: So I just thought I'd ask you what that meant.
H: It means love.
I: What's love? What does it mean to you? Can you give me a picture of it? Give me an example, a story?
H: Buddies.
I: Buddies? So God is a buddy.
H: No, he's love. God—is—love.
I: All right, where did you learn that? At school? Sunday school? Is that what the teachers told you?
H: I just thought it up.

This delightful interview demonstrates clearly the struggle of the concrete-operational child with abstract ideas and the difficulty he finds in trying to make meaning out of what he has been taught. In another example, during this past Christmas season fourth-grader Teresa became very disturbed with the idea that Jesus had two fathers—Joseph and God. She asked her teachers, "But how could this be, unless Mary got a divorce?" No amount of explanation seemed to alleviate her confusion.

Hank did not seem to be bothered by his confusion. He had learned the content well, as had Carlie who was cued that the two pieces of clay contained the same amount of clay. But Teresa was very upset, because there was a real inconsistency between content and her understanding of reality. This kind of experience may well be the source of much rejection of the Christian faith by persons of any age. Rather than helping persons find meaning, symbols sometimes can introduce irreconcilable conflicts.

To have meaning for the child at Stage 2, symbols must

have a literal, concrete referent. God is ordinarily perceived in some human form. Yet the referent itself may radically distort the intended meaning. To Teresa, God equaled father, and because she brought her own concrete constructions of family relationships to this symbol, the meaning of the biblical story was seriously distorted. The meaning of any symbol for a particular individual involves their structure, content, and feelings which are grounded in it.

Janie at age 5 demonstrates dramatically how Stage 1 functions as the basis for interpretation of Matthew 12:9-14.[5]

Interviewer: "Jesus left that place and went to one of their meeting places. A man was there who had a crippled hand." Now you tell me, what is a crippled hand? Do you remember?

Janie: Uh huh. It's a hand like that. (*She holds her hand in a rigid distorted position*).

I: All bent up? It doesn't work right, does it?

J: Yeah, it doesn't.

I: "There were some men present who wanted to accuse Jesus of wrong doing. So they asked him, 'Is it against our law to cure on the Sabbath?' " What's the law? You told me a while ago.

J: It's a thing you're not supposed to do, you're not supposed to break the law.

I: Why, what happens if you break the law?

J: You get in trouble.

I: "Jesus answered, 'What if one of you has a sheep and it falls into a deep hole on the Sabbath? Will you not take hold of it and lift it out? And a man is worth much more than a sheep!' " What did you say? Why did you think a sheep was worth more than a man?

J: 'Cause it can make clothes.

I: You think a man might ever be worth more than a sheep?

J: Never.

231

I: Never? What if a man could make clothes? Would he be worth as much as a sheep then?

J: They would both be much more than a girl.

I: Why?

J: Oh, no . . . much more than a horse.

I: Why a horse?

J: Because . . . they can make clothes.

I: A horse can't make clothes?

J: A horse *can't*.

I. "So then Jesus said. 'Our law does allow us to help someone on the Sabbath.' Then he said to the man, 'Stretch out your hand.' He stretched it out, and it became well again, just like the other one. The Pharisees left and made plans against Jesus to kill him." Jesus broke the law, didn't he? You thought that was all right?

J: It's all right 'cause Jesus is the boss.

I: That means when you act like the boss, like you were doing a little while ago, you can break the law? That makes it all right? You don't get in trouble then?

J: I don't, 'cause I'm the boss.

I: Then, do you know what those guys the Pharisees did? Those were the guys that Jesus was talking to. "They left and went out to make plans against Jesus, to kill him." The Pharisees were going to kill Jesus because he broke the law. Even though you thought he was the boss, the Pharisees didn't think so.

J: That's bad, they were going to kill Jesus.

I: You think they're bad to kill Jesus?

J: YES. He's a good guy. I love Jesus.

I: You love Jesus, do you? But the Pharisees didn't love Jesus.

J: I know, they hated him.

I: Why did they hate him?

J: Because he broke the law.

I: Because he was the boss that was all right?

J: Uh huh.

232

I: Would it be all right for the Pharisees to break the law?

J: No way. They're not the boss.

I hope it is becoming clear that we cannot extract religious concepts from a person's world-view and say, "This is religious faith." Rather, it is a person's cognitive structure that functions like a keyhole and shapes all the experiences and learnings that stimulate that person to make sense of the world and to find meaning in it.

In this section I have given examples of how different individuals have engaged in interpretation and how the meanings they construct are related to their stages. In the next section, I suggest a few of the questions that this data raises and describe some of the ways in which we are beginning to find answers.

APPLYING DEVELOPMENTAL THEORY TO INTERPRETATION

The relationship of developmental theory to interpretation raises questions about teaching in the church:

—What do we expect people to "get" from the Bible?

—How do we select biblical texts and concepts for each age or stage?

—Can children participate meaningfully in religious symbols? Can we help all ages to experience them with growing meaning?

—How does my social perspective as instructor influence what and how I teach?

My major concern is with the finding of meaning, rather than the acquisition of content without meaning. The examples I give in this section are set within that context. Those of us who have been working with cognitive developmental theory for several years have lived with more questions than answers when it comes to ways of applying the theory to teaching. But progress is taking place, and I will be sharing some of my experiences. A couple of years ago I came up with the idea of the developmental interpretation grid, described in chapter 11, and have found it to be a most useful tool. In this next section I describe its use with biblical material and religious symbols.

THE DEVELOPMENTAL INTERPRETATION GRID AND BIBLICAL INTERPRETATION

At about the same time that Janie was interviewed and scored at Stage 2, I read her the story of "The Prodigal Son." We used the colorful illustrated booklet from *Today's English Version*, which she found intriguing.[6] After she had heard the story, I asked her questions. Here is a transcription of the conversation.

Interviewer: Why do you suppose the younger brother went away and spent all his money?

Janie: I don't know . . . probably 'cause he wanted just to have something.

I: Do you think he should have done that?

J: No.

I: Why not?

J: I think that older brother was really mad, and he should have deserved that.

I: Why do you think he should deserve it?

J: Because he was the one that worked hard and everything. So he should have deserved the prizes and stuff, 'cause he worked hard, and his other brother just went out and spended all the money and selled the property and stuff.

I: Do you think the father was being fair?

J: No.

I: Why not?

J: Because . . . ummmmm . . . he let the younger brother have all the stuff, he just went out and spended all his money and stuff, and the older brother worked hard and *everything*.

I: Do you think it's important to be fair?

J: Yeah.

I: Why do you think that?

J: I don't know, 'cause it isn't fair if you don't.

I: How do you feel if your mom and dad isn't fair?

J: Sad . . . Like nobody cares about me or nothing.

I: Do you think it's all right to be unfair to somebody you don't like?

J: No! Not even them.

I: Why not?

J: Because . . . like you don't share to somebody . . . and then they have maybe the right to not share back to you and if you did that you'd be a nicer person, if you did share and they didn't.

I: Why do you think Jesus told that story?

J: Jesus?

I: Yeah, Jesus told that story.

J: He did?

I: Yeah, way back in Bible times. Remember, I started out with, I said, "Jesus went on to say." He told that story to some of the Pharisees. Why do you suppose he told that about the father?

J: *(Very emphatic) I don't know why.*

I: How do you think the younger brother felt when he'd been bad and he came home, and his father put on the big party for him and loved him. How do you think that made him feel?

J: Happy.

I: When you've been bad and then somebody loves you, it makes you feel happy?

J: Uh huh. *(yes)*

I: What do you suppose Jesus was trying to say? Let's see, how did the story end . . . "We had to have a feast and be happy because your brother was lost and now he's found."

J: Why does it stay like that? (Referring to the tape recorder. She changed the subject, and that ended the interview.)

235

Janie was able to end the conversation when it became too complex for her. Each time I have reread this interview, I have thought about how many children in how many church school classes have been unable to end such experiences except by turning off their minds or diverting their attention to more meaningful activities such as poking one another or breaking pencils.

X What immediately stood out for Janie in this parable was the unfair treatment of the elder son. This would be an expected response at Stage 2. She could focus *separately* on the father's treatment of the younger son, but to put together the father's two apparently conflicting behaviors, and to see some point to it all that might relate to Jesus, was cognitively beyond her capability. I suppose if she were asked to give the story a title it might be something like "The Unfair Father."

Many of the parables are not simple little stories intended to be used as entertainment or moral examples. The parable of The Prodigal Son presents a *reversal* of our usual expectations that the good shall be rewarded, and the bad shall be punished. There is more rejoicing over the bad penny that turns up than over the one in the pocket. Even when put in the context of Jesus' reply to the Pharisees and scribes who were criticizing him, we are still left with a nagging feeling of unfairness that suggests that our world-view is being challenged.[7]

Before I taught this parable to a group of senior highs I charted it on a developmental interpretation grid, using Stages 2 and 3. Some senior highs are at Stage 2, the same as Janie at age 6, but there is a major difference in other development. Senior highs can role-take the younger son and his desire to get away from home, Janie could not. This variation can be understood from the developmental model of Erik H. Erikson and can be added to the interpretation grid.[8]

I chose the concepts to put across the top of the grid after a careful study of the text. (If the instructor is using prepared curriculum materials, it is important to be thoroughly acquainted with whatever background study is provided for teachers.) I then drew upon the categories of the developmental theories to determine which ones fit most appropriately with the concepts in the parable. My final step was to fill in the grid with key ideas (see figure 1).

I have found that it is not necessary to be able to fill in all the spaces, or even to feel sure about the categories one has selected. The process of struggling with the text in terms of developmental theory raises many of the appropriate kinds of questions and implications of how or whether one will teach a particular text.

The grid brings out the kinds of problems that Janie did in fact encounter with the parable. It also suggests that adolescents at Stage 2 might have a point of contacting meaning that Janie did not have: empathy with the younger son leaving home. In a subsequent session with the senior highs, I decided to focus on feelings and role-taking and allow meanings to emerge at that level from personal encounters with the text. Working in small groups, the students used long pieces of shelf paper to tell the story of the *feelings* of the characters. They did this by cutting or tearing colored paper into blobs or symbols of an appropriate color and pasting them to the shelf paper. When the "stories" were completed, the group members talked about the meanings of their symbols. I am not sure that there was much understanding of the reversal or how this parable was used by Jesus and for what purpose. But I think it became related in a positive way to where these senior highs were in their own lives, whereas for Janie the parable was a confusing experience. These are the kinds of results that were also predicted by the interpretation grid.

An additional source of information for the grid is the work of Dr. Ronald Goldman of England. He has conducted research into children's understandings of religious concepts related to the logical reasoning model of Piaget. His two books are significant contributions to

DEVELOPMENTAL INTERPRETATION GRID
FOR THE PARABLE OF THE PRODIGAL SON (LUKE 15:11-32)

MODEL/ THEORY	STAGE LEVEL PERIODS	CONCEPTS, ISSUES, SYMBOLS, IMAGES, ETC.				
		Younger son: leaving home, wasteful, etc.	Older son: obedient, angry	Father: treatment of younger son	Father: treatment of older son	Reversal of expectations
Logical Reasoning	Concrete					Cannot coordinate roles of father and sons
	Formal					Can coordinate roles
Social Perspective Role-taking	Stage 2	None in preadolescence. Yes in adolescence.	Yes, related to obedience and anger	Yes, feelings of being loved	Unfair and not understood	Centers on older brother
	Stage 3	Little in preadolescence. Yes in adolescence.	Yes	First-order role-taking; may be able to see each person from other's point of view		Can coordinate roles, see some obvious implications
Moral Reasoning — Persons	Stage 2	Bad	Good; anger justified	Good	Bad	
	Stage 3	Bad in preadolescence. Okay in adolescence.	Good; could have been more understanding	Good, loving, concerned	Questionable	
Moral Reasoning — Justice	Stage 2	Preadolescent: deserves punishment.	Deserves reward	Undeserved but appreciated	Unfair	Not understood, unjust; focus on unfairness
	Stage 3	Already punished by no food, etc.	Deserves reward	Okay, because son already suffered	Unfair, but son should understand	Tendency to compartmentalize with focus on father's forgiveness of younger son.

Figure 1

238

the relationship between developmental theory and religious thinking. Using a series of interviews in which children respond to pictures and to biblical texts, he has documented how children and youth think about a variety of religious concepts and symbols. In his first book, *Religious Thinking from Childhood to Adolescence*, he includes a wealth of quotations and material on implications.[9]

His second book, *Readiness for Religion*, describes a curriculum for developmental religious education. One of his major themes is the dualism he uncovered in his interviews, a "dualistic system which separates religion from the rest of life."[10] One of his interviewees is described in this way:

He evinces a great deal of confusion about these scripture stories, being unable to transcend their concrete imagery and language and as a result accepts them at a literal level, although plainly dissatisfied with his explanations. . . .He solves these and other problems mainly by ignoring them and by beginning to separate "the religious" from the rest of experience.

His descriptions are compatible with the experiences we have had in our research. In order to work toward solving these problems, Goldman has edited a curriculum for religious education entitled "Readiness for Religion" which is consistent with his proposals in the book by that title.[11] In units published as sets of booklets, he deals with such subjects as Sheep and Shepherds, Bread, Symbols, and What Is the Bible? A major emphasis is the study of biblical symbols in order to build a foundation for meaningful understanding of the Bible when one reaches older adolescence and adulthood.

SYMBOLS AND THE DEVELOPMENTAL INTERPRETATION GRID

Much of our participation in the life of a religious community is in the realm of the symbolic. Use of developmental theory can enable such participation to become more significant for the persons involved. The

Developmental Journey

reenactment of Jesus' last supper with his disciples is a
focal symbolic act or ritual in Christian churches whether
it be called The Lord's Supper or Communion or The
Eucharist. To explore its meaning developmentally, it can
be divided into its component symbols such as table,
community, bread, cup, thanksgiving, and forgiveness of
sins. Or it can be looked at as a whole, as a total symbolic

DEVELOPMENTAL INTERPRETATION GRID

MODEL/ THEORY	STAGE/ LEVEL PERIOD	CONCEPTS, ISSUES, SYMBOLS, IMAGES, ETC.
		Lord's Supper, Communion
Faith Role of Symbol	Stage 1	Concrete, may center on one aspect (cup, loaf, pastor); magical qualities.
	Stage 2	Symbol is equivalent to the reality: Lord's Supper is the literal reenactment of Jesus' last meal with his disciples; it tells a true story.
	Stage 3	Understanding of some abstract meanings (love, forgiveness). Personal relationship with Jesus. Good feeling important. A sense of community associated with church friends and with Jesus. Importance of remembrance of what happened and its meaning. Meaning not separated from the ritual itself.
	Stage 4	Can separate abstract meanings from the ritual itself; the ritual may be seen as a channel for experiencing the divine, for communicating forgiveness, for transmitting the Judeo-Christian heritage as a system of beliefs.
	Stage 5	The complexity of meanings of the heritage and tradition may come together in relationship to the self as seen in the ongoing flow of life and lives.

ritual. I am going to take it in this last form and put it on the developmental interpretation grid, analyzing it from the standpoint of the Role of Symbol. The content of the grid may vary somewhat according to different traditions. The descriptions come from my own understandings. The intent is not to focus on those, but is rather to convey the increasing complexity and depth of meaning through the stages.

The concreteness of symbolic objects and rituals, and the universal appeal of good stories, means that these are readily available as tools to help persons incorporate religious meaning into their life journeys. We need to take them seriously in planning worship and education in the church. Incorporating these with the understandings gained from the grid opens up creative possibilities for experiencing traditional symbols. In Appendix C, I have included a lesson plan for an intergenerational event intended to explore some of the meanings of communion. It utilizes the four elements of the confluent education model and emphasizes Stage 2 and Stage 3 understandings of symbol. I have discovered that concentrating on concrete images is often very revealing and informative for adults whose major exposure has been verbal and abstract. It is my informed guess that symbolic statements tend to narrow down and encapsulate meaning, whereas symbolic objects, acts, and stories are more likely to open up new insights. Verbal statements help us maintain a structure or system of beliefs. Active participation with objects, actions, and stories may tend to crack it open. Probably we need to keep the two in tension. And above all, we may need to struggle with the meanings that are mediated by symbols, the shaping visions that shine through, recognizing our own limitations and that for the moment we may "see in a mirror dimly."[13]

SUMMARY OF CORRELATIONS

Earlier in this chapter I raised some questions that grew out of the correlations between cognitive developmental theory and biblical interpretation. If there are limits to understanding determined by stage structure, then we must accept that there will always be "distortions" of religious concepts and that it may be impossible to come to any agreement on what the "real" meanings are. The shaping vision is not easily pinned down! But this does not suggest that we can be irresponsible in our use of biblical and symbolic material. We need to treat both the material and the students in a way that honors their integrity. I use a four-step procedure in my own preparation for teaching.

The first step is the instructor's own study of the material. This may mean a careful exploration of what a biblical text actually says, what it meant at the time it was written, and what it might mean today. The instructor can find it especially helpful to reflect upon personal meanings that emerge for him or her as a result of this responsible study of the material. If this is not done, it may be difficult to involve students in a search for meaning. If prepared materials are being used, this is the step at which suggested background study should be considered carefully.

The second step is to prepare a developmental interpretation grid. This requires a disciplined attempt to focus on concepts and then role-take them from the students' perspective.

The third step is to make some decisions about the use of the material. Sometimes it may seem necessary to drop a particular subject completely if it is apt to be confusing or thoroughly distorted. For instance, I think that I would teach The Lost Sheep rather than The Prodigal Son to children because it does not present concrete contradictions. Or the decision may be to focus on one or two concepts rather than the six or eight that are possible as long as this does not do an injustice to the material.

The fourth step is then to plan the specific format for the

class session, first deciding upon purpose or goals and then developing activities appropriate to that purpose and to the concepts in the lesson.

This procedure is clearly time-consuming, and even the most conscientious instructor is not going to be able to follow it faithfully. I have found that to struggle with it, whenever possible, gradually builds skills that carry over into the times when my preparation must be sketchy. And recognizing the tentativeness of my own understandings reminds me to listen with sensitivity to students rather than to push for "correct" meanings.

In our concern to teach abstract concepts about the Christian faith, perhaps we have forgotten that Jesus is the concrete expression of God's love and mercy and justice. Both developmental theory and Sanders' sequence for asking questions suggest that it is necessary to start with the concrete. Keeping this in mind the instructor can communicate effectively, even on those occasions when preparation time has not been adequate, by focusing on concrete symbols and experiences.

PRACTICAL ACTIVITIES AND RELIGIOUS CONCEPTS

In chapters 10 and 11 I have described an educational model and a number of activities that help stimulate thinking, development, and learning. Exercises at the end of some of the chapters also suggest additional activities. Many of these were first developed in religious education settings. In this section I describe some activities that relate specifically to the content of the Christian religion.

ROLE-PLAYING
Role-taking is a critical factor in the developmental journey and is of special concern within the context of the Christian religion. Here is an example of a strategy that combines a biblical text and stimulation in role-taking ability.

Role-Play of Matthew 12:9-14

Purpose: To develop an understanding of the social perspective of the Pharisees as it appears in this text.

Materials: Copies of Matthew 12:1-14 plus information about the Pharisees

Role-play instructions and questions on newsprint or chalkboard or duplicated copies

Instructions: Help participants form into groups of five or six persons each. Give each group copies of the biblical text and provide instructions and questions as follows:

"In your group, choose two interviewers, and the rest will be Pharisees. The interviewers will meet together, apart from the Pharisees, to study the text and the suggested questions, and decide how to question the Pharisees. The Pharisees will study the text and decide how they will answer questions from the interviewers. You may develop a contemporary situation, but stick with the basic ideas stated in the text."

Suggested Questions

After reading the text—use Matthew 12:9-14 only—consider the following questions that the interviewers are to ask the Pharisees.

1. What are you called?
2. What does your title mean? What are your responsibilities?
3. Where did you meet Jesus?
4. What question did you ask Jesus?
5. Why are you so concerned about the law?
6. Why did it upset you when Jesus healed the man?
7. What would happen if everyone followed Jesus' example and broke the law?
8. Does Jesus fit your idea of the Messiah? Why or why not?

Role-plays can be done informally in each group, or each group can be asked to present the role-play in front of the entire group. The latter is more threatening and time-consuming, but if this is done, tell the groups that you will cut them off when it appears that they have exhausted possibilities, or that they should feel free to take this action themselves.

Follow the role-plays with group discussion. Suggested questions:
1. How did the Pharisees feel in their roles? Why?
2. How did the interviewers feel in their roles? Why?

Ask other questions that will make clear the role of the Pharisees as defenders of the order and structure of the faith, rather than as the traditional bad guys.

The information about the Pharisees to be supplied with the text is:

Pharisees: In New Testament times, the Pharisees were members of the largest and most influential Jewish sect. (Other Jewish sects were the Sadducees, the Essenes, and the Zealots.) The sect of the Pharisees originated in the second century B.C. in protest over collaboration between some Jews and the Greek rulers. Their religion centered on strict and detailed conformity with the law and the oral tradition. They were concerned to support and maintain these against the encroachment of Greek customs.

This strategy involves the enactive, the emotional, the verbal-rational, and perhaps a change in mental image (of the Pharisees). It may contribute new content for some people, a new way of looking at the Pharisees. It may involve the stimulation of a new social perspective for others as it gives experience in taking the point of view of others.

I have used this strategy in conjunction with biblical study and as an introduction to Stage 4 social perspective in courses on cognitive developmental theory.

VALUES CLARIFICATION

Values-clarification strategies are effective tools to introduce almost any subject. Some of the examples that follow have been used in specific contexts. In cases where they have been used in relation to a specific subject, this is indicated in parentheses.

Values Voting

—How many of you think it is *ever* all right to break the law?

—How many of you think the Ten Commandments should be revised in the light of contemporary understandings?

—How many of you think that the Genesis creation story and the theory of evolution are in serious conflict with one another?

(The next two questions have been used to introduce the two versions of the Parable of the Lost Sheep, Luke 15:1-7 and Matthew 18:1-15.)

—How many of you think a teacher should spend a whole class session helping one slow learner, leaving the rest of the class to its own devices?

—How many of you think a teacher should spend the total class session helping one student who has deliberately been absent from the previous three sessions?

Values Continuum

—Are you more like *Believing Belinda* who accepts all her religious beliefs without any question, or like *Prove-It-To-Me Prosper* who demands proof before he accepts any religious belief or idea?

—Are you more like *Literal Linda* who takes everything in the Bible as literally true, or like *Bible-Burning Bernie* who sees the Bible as literature but without any religious significance?

—How much freedom do you have? More like *Restricted Rita*, all decisions made for her, or like

Free-As-A-Bird Fred who has complete freedom to choose for himself? (This one was used in a study of II Corinthians 5:16-17.)

—Are you more like *Do-Your-Thing Donna* who questions rules, does what she wants, does the unexpected, or more like *Obedient Obadiah* who follows all rules, does what is expected at home, work, and church. (This was used to introduce a study of The Prodigal Son.)

In using values clarification, it is important to ask "why" questions and to emphasize reasons. This stimulates thinking, and, as people hear one another's reasons, it may also stimulate development in role-taking and other aspects of cognitive development.

MORAL DILEMMAS

Moral dilemmas raise issues that are also encountered in biblical materials. I have used the Heinz dilemma to introduce the study of Matthew 12:9-14 and in relationship to Paul and his struggles with the law. My colleague, H. Edward Everding, has used Dilemma I—the story of Joe and his father (Appendix A)—in conjunction with the Parable of the Unjust Steward.

Rather than talking *about* issues from a detached point of view, moral dilemmas enable participants to enter into the subject matter at a personal level. Such experiences encourage thinking rather than "right answers" and help persons to explore personal meanings.

GENERAL

The examples of activities that I have given are not meant to be exhaustive but rather to open up possibilities. A particular strategy must always emerge from the instructor's understanding of the concepts and the goals for teaching a particular piece of material. The lesson plan in Appendix C provides some additional activities that relate to understandings of the Last Supper.

Much of my experience in recent years has been with youth and adults, rather than with children. The suggestions I have given in this chapter are generally appropriate for older age groups, although some can be adapted for children. New curriculum materials for children and youth are making use of values-clarification strategies and many options are offered. It may be very helpful for the teacher to see these in the context of development and confluent education rather than simply as activities to keep students busy or interested.

Resources for youth and adults are listed in the notes.[14]

REACHING PEOPLE

One of the shaping visions of most religious communities embodies the dimension of caring about persons. One way of expressing this caring is to take the role of other individuals in the community, to try to see issues from their points of view. Cognitive developmental theory is a tool that may help us grow in the direction of making this shaping vision a reality. In this section I suggest some specific areas that can give us insights into this concern.

PERCEPTIONS OF COMMUNITY/SOCIETY

A church or religious body is a community of persons, committed to common goals or visions. These goals or visions are embodied in the structure of the institution.

This brief definition encompasses three stages in its understanding of community/society, one of the factors of social perspective:

—a community of persons (the interpersonal structure of Stage 3)

—common goals or visions (the triadic structure of Stage 4)

—goals or visions embodied in the structure (principles of Stage 5)

Cognitive developmental theory tells us that most adults understand the church from the perspectives of

Stage 3 and/or Stage 4. Only a few perceive it at the principled level. This means that the church is important to many persons in terms of confirming those world-views already held (whether relativistic or absolutistic), and that it is perceived more as a community of persons in interpersonal relationships than as an institution with common visions and decision-making procedures. At Stage 3, symbols are closely bound with the reality toward which they point. Therefore any tampering with symbols may seem to destroy that reality. Changes in a worship service, in rituals, or in the arrangement of furniture in the sanctuary may be experienced as tampering with faith itself. Understanding this, leaders of religious traditions and congregations can be more sensitive to their constituencies when changes are contemplated.

On the other hand, persons at Stage 4 often are searching for a knowledgeable understanding of their religious tradition. They may downplay feelings in favor of rational insights. They may be in the process of reappropriating traditional symbols, of rejecting their old meanings, of trying to make sense of them in new ways. A change in symbolic rituals may offer them opportunities for the acquisition of fresh meaning.

High school students at Stage 3 may be communicated with through peer group, significant adults, and feelings. The *content* to which they respond is extremely variable. Some may be attracted to conservative theological positions, others to radical political movements. The same is true of adults. The religious institution needs to take seriously the meaning *structure* of its constituency if it hopes to communicate its shaping visions and express and enact those visions in appropriate ways.[15]

One of my students at the Iliff School of Theology decided to try to express the concepts of his sermons in Stage 3 and 4 understandings. After six weeks of consciously making this attempt, he walked into the meeting of the church board and received a standing ovation, a tribute to the tremendous sermons he had preached in the previous few weeks! I do not know how he changed his sermons, and this result is probably more than can usually be expected, but it is a striking example of what can happen when one takes seriously the world-view of other persons.

The social perspective stage of persons has a strong influence on how they experience the democratic decision-making procedures that are a part of many religious bodies. Some of these implications were described in chapter 9. At lower stages, persons may become very impatient with decision-making, evaluation, and planning processes because they are not able to see the importance of such processes. At higher stages, persons may become equally impatient with the bypassing of democratic procedures.

The religious body can be the community of both support and challenge to its membership.[16] Awareness of cognitive developmental theory among the leadership helps to facilitate these functions. If curriculum materials for grade school children require abstract thinking and Stage 4 understandings, there will be neither support nor challenge for those children. Experiences within the church community may be largely meaningless. If adults at Stage 4 are searching for clear definitions of common visions from among rational choices, but receive simplistic answers that are either relativistic or absolutistic, they will be neither supported nor challenged. And yet these same answers are what may be needed at Stage 3!

As I near the end of this chapter and of the book, I am aware that many questions are raised and not answered, and that there may be frustration on the part of the reader. I am sure that this chapter could, and perhaps should, be expanded into another book. This will have to wait until more experience and research have fed into what it might mean to take cognitive developmental theory seriously in the context of religion and religious institutions.

MISUSES

The major misuse of cognitive developmental theory in the religious context has been, and will continue to be, the stage labeling of persons according to behavior and/or theological position. Certain psychological and theological approaches may appeal to certain stages. This does not mean that everyone who subscribes to those approaches is at that stage, nor does it mean that everyone at that stage responds positively to certain approaches. Content can be a powerful determinant in what attracts individuals.

In Jack Pressau's recently published book *I'm Saved, You're Saved . . . Maybe*, Kohlberg's stages are related to certain theological positions in a way that does not appear to have any validation in research. For instance, Stage 4 salvation is equated with evangelical programs and Stage 5 with social liberalism, ecumenical concerns, and process theology.[17] Our research indicates that adults from Stage 2(3) through Stage 5 may find meaning in any of these concerns (content), although their interpretations may vary widely. It also appears that a process mode of thinking appears prior to stage 4 of moral reasoning, thus enabling complex interpretations of Process Theology and other content.[18] I cannot stress strongly enough the dangers of equating stages with particular interests or positions, even if research should eventually indicate some valid connections. Such labeling can result in the unjust stereotyping of both individuals and theological points of view.

THE SHAPING VISION

The shaping visions of a tradition are what give it its ultimate power in the lives of persons. Translating these visions into meaningful experiences for each age and stage is a challenge for cognitive developmental theory. We have seen how role-taking, as expressed in the Golden Rule, is transformed at each stage into something which only approximates its shaping vision; and yet, the vision continues to shape understanding except where it seems to disappear at Stage 1, when role-taking is extremely limited.

The image of the funnel is an appropriate one for expressing what happens to the shaping vision as it narrows from its most complex expression to the least complex (figure 2). If the funnel remains fairly straight then the shaping vision can be understood with some integrity, but if it veers to one side, its meaning is distorted. Then as an individual grows in understanding, the widening funnel leads not toward the shaping vision but toward a serious distortion of it (figure 3).

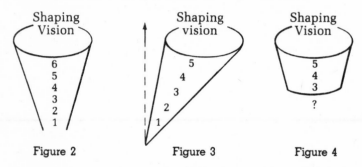

Figure 2   Figure 3   Figure 4

Or the funnel can be cut off, and the shaping vision may disappear (figure 4). For instance, in the story of Jesus and the Pharisees, the shaping vision of Jesus' resolution of the conflict between law and life seems to lose its power at Stage 3, when distortion destroys the original meaning.

These insights, which I offer in a tentative way, challenge us to examine our understandings of Bible and faith in the light of what the shaping visions might be and encourage us to diligently explore how we might help others to find meaning.

From **The Way of the Sufi**
IDRIES SHAH

MOSES AND THE SHEPHERD

No man can understand more than his whole mind is capable of understanding; and for this reason it has been truly said: "Speak to every man according to his understanding." As each man can perceive, so will he benefit.

It is related that Moses called a humble shepherd a blasphemer, because he heard the poor man offering to comb God's hair, wash His robe and kiss His hand.

God admonished Moses, indirectly teaching him . . . that the shepherd had not the . . . experience to realize that Moses was talking about an incorporeal deity. "Thus hast thou driven away a worshipper from the nearest to Me that he could approach. There is a gradation in all men: each will perceive what he can perceive, and at the stage at which he can perceive it."[19]

POSTSCRIPT

One reason people are different is that they have different world-views based in their cognitive structures. Understanding this helps us to accept all persons as they are. Taking this seriously, persons become ends as we try to put ourselves in the place of others.

If this makes sense to you, you have learned the most important thing about cognitive developmental theory, and are participating in the purpose of this book.

APPENDIX A

MORAL JUDGMENT INTERVIEW

Dilemma III: In Europe, a woman was near death from a special kind of cancer. There was one drug that the doctors thought might save her. It was a form of radium that a druggist in the same town had recently discovered. The drug was expensive to make, but the druggist was charging ten times what the drug cost him to make. He paid $200 for the radium and charged $2,000 for a small dose of the drug. The sick woman's husband, Heinz, went to everyone he knew to borrow the money, but he could only get together about $1,000, which is half of what it cost. He told the druggist that his wife was dying, and asked him to sell it cheaper or let him pay later. But the druggist said, "No, I discovered the drug and I'm going to make money from it." So Heinz gets desperate and considers breaking into the man's store to steal the drug for his wife.

1. Should Heinz steal the drug?
1a. Why or why not?
2. If Heinz doesn't love his wife, should he steal the drug for her?
2a. Why or why not?
3. Suppose the person dying is not his wife but a stranger. Should Heinz steal the drug for the stranger?
3a. Why or why not?
4. (*If* you favor stealing the drug for a stranger.) Suppose it's a pet animal he loves. Should Heinz steal to save the pet animal?

4a. Why or why not?
5. Is it important for people to do everything they can to save another's life?
5a. Why or why not?
6. It is against the law for Heinz to steal. Does that make it morally wrong?
6a. Why or why not?
7. Should people try to do everything they can to obey the law?
7a. Why or why not?
7b. How does this apply to what Heinz should do?

Dilemma III': Heinz did break into the store. He stole the drug and gave it to his wife. In the newspapers the next day, there was an account of the robbery. Mr. Brown, a police officer who knew Heinz, read the account. He remembered seeing Heinz running away from the store and realized that it was Heinz who stole the drug. Mr. Brown wonders whether he should report that Heinz was the robber.

1. Should Officer Brown report Heinz for stealing?
1a. Why or why not?
2. Officer Brown finds and arrests Heinz. Heinz is brought into court, and a jury is selected. The jury's job is to find whether a person is innocent or guilty of committing a crime. The jury finds Heinz guilty. It is up to the judge to determine the sentence. Should the judge give Heinz some sentence, or should he suspend the sentence and let Heinz go free?
2a. Why or why not?
3. Thinking in terms of society, why should people who break the law be punished?
3a. How does this apply to what Heinz should do?
4. Heinz was doing what his conscience told him when he stole the drug. Should a law-breaker be punished if he is acting out of conscience?
4a. Why or why not?

Dilemma I: Joe is a fourteen-year-old boy who wanted to go to camp very much. His father promised him he could go if he saved up the money for it himself. So Joe worked hard at his paper route and saved up the $40 it cost to go to camp and a little more besides. But just before camp was going to start, his father changed his mind. Some of his friends decided to go on a special fishing trip, and Joe's father was short of the money it would cost. So he told Joe to give him the money he had saved from the paper route. Joe didn't want to give up going to camp, so he thinks of refusing to give his father the money.

1.   Should Joe refuse to give his father the money?
1a. Why or why not?
2.   Is the fact that Joe earned the money himself the most important thing in the situation?
2a. Why or why not?
3.   The father promised Joe he could go to camp if he earned the money. Is the fact that the father promised the most important thing in the situation?
3a. Why or why not?
4.   Why in general should a promise be kept?
5.   Is it important to keep a promise to someone you don't know well and probably won't see again?
5a. Why or why not?
6.   What do you think is the most important thing a son should be concerned about in his relationship to his father?
6a. Why is that the most important thing?
7.   What do you think is the most important thing a father should be concerned about in his relationship to his son?
7a. Why is that the most important thing?

—From *Assessing Moral Stages: A Manual*, Part III
By Lawrence Kohlberg, Anne Colby, John Gibbs,
Betsy Speicher-Dubin, and Clark Power Harvard
University (Partially complete) August, 1977

APPENDIX B

MATTHEW 12:9-14 (RSV)

And [Jesus] went on from there, [he had been with his disciples in the grainfields] and entered their synagogue. And behold, there was a man with a withered hand. And they asked him, "Is it lawful to heal on the sabbath?" so that they might accuse him. [The Pharisees thought it was not lawful.] He said to them, "What man of you, if he has one sheep and it falls into a pit on the sabbath, will not lay hold of it and lift it out? Of how much more value is a man than a sheep! So it is lawful to do good on the sabbath." Then he said to the man, "Stretch out your hand." And the man stretched it out, and it was restored, whole like the other. But the Pharisees went out and took counsel against him, how to destroy him.

QUESTIONS
1. What do you think of that story? Why do you suppose that Jesus did that? What do you think the whole story means?
2. Are there words you don't understand?
3. Should Jesus have broken the law? Why?
4. Which is worse, breaking the law or not healing someone? Why?
5. Which is more important or of more value, a sheep or a man? Why?
6. Would it be as right to break the law for a sheep as for a man? Why?
7. Would it be as right for the Pharisees to break the law as for Jesus to do it? Why?
8. What would happen if everybody broke the law?

9. Thinking in terms of society, were the Pharisees justified in being upset with Jesus? Why? What reasons might they give for being upset?
10. What do you think the value of life meant to Jesus?

—From "Report of a Research Project on Implications of Kohlberg's Theory of Moral Reasoning for Biblical Interpretation" by H. Edward Everding and Mary M. Wilcox, November, 1975, p. 27.

APPENDIX C

LEADERS: Planned and led by Barbara Amori, Kris Tierney, Mary Wilcox

PURPOSE: To explore some of the meanings of the sacrament of communion.

CONCEPTS: communion
Last Supper/remembrance
table/community
cup/promise/covenant
celebration

GOALS: To help the participants to
1. experience community around the table and to reflect on its meaning.
2. express what they know about communion.
3. learn some facts about the Last Supper.
4. experience some of the feeling of the Last Supper.
5. discover some reasons for understanding communion as celebration.
6. relate to a picture or image of Jesus.
7. celebrate with food and music.

OBJECTIVES: The participants will be able to
1. Draw pictures of the tables at which they usually eat and of the people who eat with them.
2. Share with others at their table what they feel about the experience they have drawn.
3. Stand by a sign describing how they would enjoy celebrating their birthdays.
4. Verbally list what they know and can remember about communion.

261

5. Choose the picture of Jesus most like their ideas of him.
6. Experience walking to the Last Supper.
7. Participate in a guided fantasy of the Last Supper and share some feelings about the experience.
8. Eat and sing.

MATERIALS:

six tables with six chairs each
table paper and crayons
newsprint instructions
signs
words of song on newsprint
communion cup
food (grapes, cheese, etc.)
guitar music

easel

tables

ROOM SET-UP:

arrange tables radially
have a box or basket of crayons on each table which is covered with table paper
pictures of Jesus on bulletin board
communion cup on display
easel and newsprint with instructions
signs posted in three places

Time	Activities

8:45 a.m.   Ask early arrivals to help set out food on plates and to examine posted pictures of Jesus.

9:00
I. Work at tables

    a. As people enter, guide them to tables. Make sure that each table has a mixture of ages.

    b. Point out the directions on the newsprint: "On the table paper, draw a picture of the table where you usually eat.

Draw the people around the table who usually eat with you.

Choose a color that shows how you usually feel when you sit at this table. Use that color to draw a circle around your picture."

1. Emphasize that this does not need to be a work of art.

2. As people finish, suggest that they might get up and look at one another's pictures.

9:15   c. Ask the people at each table to look at one another's pictures if they have not already done so. Give everybody a chance to explain his/her picture to the other people at the table—

Introduce yourselves and give your names.

In what room is your table?

What does your choice of color mean about how you feel?

What are some different feelings about that table?

9:25   d. To celebrate your birthday, how many people would you put around that table? Point out the prepared signs posted on the wall. Signs say:

Alone	One Special Person	Several or a lot of people

1. Ask everyone to go and stand by the sign that states what they prefer.

2. Ask for some reasons for the choices.

3. Brief input: recognize differences and suggest how most of us like to do important things with other people.

9:30

II. What do we know about communion?

a. Ask: does anyone know a Bible story about Jesus eating a supper with his friends, around a table?

263

b. What do we do in church to remember that story? How many things can we remember . . . what objects do we see, what do we do?

9:35

III. Experiencing the Last Supper

a. Get up and look at the pictures of Jesus. Choose one which is most like your idea of Jesus. Keep this in your mind as we do the next activity.

b. Get everyone in a large circle and start walking in a circle.

"We've been walking all day, it is hot, we are tired . . . Walk how you walk when you feel that way . . . hot and tired . . . it feels hotter . . . you are so tired . . . your feet hurt . . . Then someone says, we are almost to the next house where we are going to eat! Suddenly you feel better and want to get there in a hurry. How will you walk? . . . There is the house . . . you are almost there . . . There are some stairs on the outside. Start to walk up those stairs. How will you walk? . . . Now you are at the top of the stairs and on a roof. Walk across the roof toward your table . . . there is a door into a little room . . . walk through the door and sit down at your table."

c. Now we are going to pretend some more, and we'll be closing our eyes. A rule in pretending this way is that if you don't want to keep pretending, just open your eyes and come back into this room. But be quiet so you don't bother the other people.

d. Guided fantasy

"Close your eyes . . . Get comfortable in your chairs . . . Relax your feet . . . your legs . . . your hands . . . your arms . . . your stomach . . . your neck. Listen to yourself breathe . . . You are sitting in that little room on the roof . . . the

264

light is very dim because there are no windows, just an open door . . . You are sitting at the table. Your friends are sitting around the table, too . . . one of them is Jesus . . . picture what Jesus looks like. . . . You feel relaxed and happy and hungry. On the table is a big basket of bread . . . a big cup shaped like a bowl, full of wine . . . other bowls with grapes and olives and nuts and some cheese. . . . Someone passes you a bowl of grapes and you take some . . . they are cool and juicy and sweet . . . feel how good they taste. . . .

"Then Jesus takes the loaf of bread and says a blessing . . . and then he starts to break off pieces and he passes the pieces to each of you . . . the bread tastes warm and fresh . . . and then Jesus says something strange, which you don't understand . . . about the bread being broken like his body is going to be . . . you begin to feel worried about what might happen to Jesus. And then he picks up the big cup of wine and says thank you to God . . . and he passes the big cup around the table and tells you to each take a drink. He says that the wine is like his blood . . . and you get more worried. But then he says that the cup of wine makes him think of the promises God has always made . . . to take care of us, to love us so much. . . . And now Jesus says that he will help you to remember God's promises and help you keep your promises to God . . . He says, 'Every time you, my friends, get together and you eat bread and drink wine, remember me and remember the promises of God . . . and your promises to God . . .'

"Now it is very quiet . . . you know that Jesus is getting ready to leave you . . . you feel both sad and happy, because you know that when you and your friends get together it will seem that Jesus is still with you. . . . Now it is time for you to leave . . . You and your friends and Jesus get up, walk out the door onto the roof, down the stairs, into the street. . . . Feel the cool evening air. . . . As you walk you are coming back to Wheat Ridge, into fellowship hall . . . to this table. . . . Move your hands . . . your feet. . . . Move around on your chair . . . hear the other people moving . . . remember who is sitting across from you . . . next to you. . . . When you feel like it, open your eyes . . . look at somebody . . . give them a smile."

   e. Debriefing

      1. How did you feel? What did you think? Get responses from group.

      2. What are the promises that Jesus talked about? What did the cup mean to him?

      3. What is there about communion that might be like a birthday party? What might make us happy? (God's promises, eating and drinking, being with good friends.)

IV. Celebration: eating

   a. Bring out food and put on tables

   b. Brief story

"There were some people in a far off land who had very stiff arms and very short spoons. They could not get the food into their own mouths. See if you can figure out how they ate and demonstrate this with someone at your table." (Feed one another.)

   c. Teach and sing one verse of "Sons of God."

9:55   d. Closing

      1. Have everybody stand and form a circle around the edge of the room, holding

266

hands. While singing the Doxology, take a few steps toward the center of the room, then a few steps back in time to the music. During the steps forward, raise hands and arms. During the steps backward, lower hands and arms.

NOTES

CHAPTER I

1. *The Watergate Hearings*, quoted by Dan Candee, "The Moral Psychology of Watergate," *Journal of Social Issues*, 31 (1975), 185.
2. Egil Krogh statement, *Ibid.*, pp. 186, 192.
3. Discussion led and recorded by the author.
4. A summary of this research was presented to the Association of Professors and Researchers in Religious Education, in November 1975, and is given in the unpublished paper, "Report of a Research Project on Implications of Kohlberg's Theory of Moral Reasoning for Biblical Interpretation" by H. Edward Everding and Mary M. Wilcox, Iliff School of Theology, 2201 South University Blvd., Denver, Colorado, 80210.
5. In one of his later works, Piaget with Inhelder includes a discussion of the affective as it relates to each period. This is found in: Jean Piaget and Bärbel Inhelder, *The Psychology of the Child* (New York: Basic Books, 1969).

CHAPTER II

1. Term created by Robert J. Rohdenburg while a graduate student at Iliff School of Theology.
2. Term used by Piaget. See J. H. Flavell, *The Developmental Psychology of Jean Piaget* (New York: Nostrand Company, 1963), p. 211.
3. Unless otherwise indicated, interview quotations are from the files of the author.
4. Monique Laurendeau and Adrien Pinard, *The Development of the Concept of Space in the Child* (New York: International Universities Press, 1970), pp. 310-402. This book contains excellent descriptions of a number of tests, including the one described on perspective, with chapters on presentation and analysis.
5. Jean Piaget, *The Child's Conception of the World* (Totowa, N.J.: Littlefield, Adams & Co., 1965), p. 220.
6. Interviews with Harry and Kathy are from the files of H. Edward Everding.
7. From the *Denver Post*, 5 November 1974, p. 1.
8. Robert L. Selman, "Social-Cognitive Understanding: A Guide to Educational and Clinical Practice," in Thomas Lickona, ed., *Moral Development and Behavior: Theory, Research and Social Issues* (New York: Holt, Rinehart and Winston, 1976), pp. 299-316. Selman

has been doing significant research in the area of role-taking related to Piagetian tasks and to Kohlberg's stages of moral reasoning. Three sources for his work are:

—"The Necessity (But Insufficiency) of Social Perspective Taking for Conceptions of Justice at Three Early Levels," (coauthor William Damon) in David J. DePalma and Jeanne M. Foley, eds., *Moral Development: Current Theory and Research* (Hillsdale, N.J.: Lawrence Erlbaum Associates, 1975), pp. 57-74.

—Robert L. Selman, *The Development of Conceptions of Interpersonal Relations* (Harvard University: Judge Baker Social Reasoning Project, 1974).

—Robert L. Selman, "Taking Another's Perspective: Role-Taking Development in Early Childhood," *Child Development*, 42 (December 1971), 1721-34.

Selman at times uses the term "social perspective taking" somewhat synonomously with "reciprocal role-taking," and not quite in the broader sense which I have used in this book.

The testing which Selman is doing measures the child's ability to "infer another's capabilities, attributes, expectations, feelings, and potential reactions. . . . Taking another's perspective implies the ability to differentiate the other's view from one's own, and the ability to shift, balance, and evaluate both perceptual and cognitive object input, all of which is clearly cognitive." Quoted from article above.

9. Art Buchwald, *Denver Post*, 30 March 1975, p. 17.

CHAPTER III

1. Jean Piaget, *Six Psychological Studies* (New York: Random House, 1967), p. 8.
2. Piaget describes both horizontal décalage and vertical décalage. Horizontal décalage means the same operation is applied to different content. Vertical décalage is the reconstruction of a structure by means of an operation from a different stage. For further reading on this see:
   —Flavell, *Developmental Psychology of Jean Piaget*, pp. 20-23.
   —Jean Piaget, *The Child and Reality* (New York: Grossman, 1973), pp. 53-54.
3. We have found that the most helpful next step for most students in the study of development of logical reasoning is to read an introduction to Piaget. Two books which have proven to be useful are:
   —Herbert Ginsburg and Sylvia Opper, *Piaget's Theory of Intellectual Development: An Introduction* (Englewood Cliffs, N.J.: Prentice-Hall, 1969).
   —Mary Ann Spencer Pulaski, *Understanding Piaget: An Introduction to Children's Cognitive Development* (New York: Harper, 1971).

   A much more difficult but thorough treatment is Flavell's book listed in note #2 above. Included is an extensive bibliography of Piaget's writings.

4. Laurendeau and Pinard, *Development of the Concept of Space*, p. 348.
5. Flavell, *Developmental Psychology of Jean Piaget*, p. 211.
6. *Denver Post*, 5 November 1974, p. 1.
7. *Denver Post*, "Open Forum," 26 August 1976, p. 23.
8. Lawrence Kohlberg and Peter Scharf, "Bureaucratic Violence and Conventional Moral Thinking," April 6, 1972, typewritten, p. 4.
9. Richard Hammer, *Court-Martial of Lieutenant Calley* (New York: Coward, McCann & Geoghegan, 1975) quoted by Kohlberg and Scharf, p. 5.
10. Kohlberg and Scharf, "Bureaucratic Violence," pp. 5-6.
11. *New York Times*, 25 November 1969, quoted in Kohlberg and Scharf, p. 5.
12. This dilemma is changed and adapted from the filmstrip:
   —"The Trouble with Truth," from the series *First Things: Sound Filmstrips for Primary Years* (Guidance Associates of Pleasantville, New York, April 1972).
13. H. Edward Everding and Mary M. Wilcox, "Implications of Kohlberg's Theory of Moral Reasoning for Biblical Interpretation" (Paper presented at the annual meeting of the Association of Professors and Researchers in Religious Education, November 1975), p. 34.

CHAPTER IV

1. Robert E. Ornstein, *The Psychology of Consciousness* (New York: Viking Press, 1972).
2. Elizabeth Leonie Simpson, "A Holistic Approach to Moral Development and Behavior," in Lickona, ed., *Moral Development and Behavior*, pp. 159-70.
3. Gary Whetstone.
4. Milton Schwebel and Jane Raph, eds., *Piaget in the Classroom* (New York: Basic Books, 1973), p. 77.
5. James Rest, "Patterns of Preference and Comprehension in Moral Judgment," *Journal of Personality*, 41 (1973), 86-109.
6. Lawrence Kohlberg, "The Cognitive-Developmental Approach to Moral Education," *Phi Delta Kappan*, (June 1975), p. 672. Also found in Scharf, pp. 36-51, see note #10.
7. Lawrence Kohlberg, et al., *Assessing Moral Stages: A Manual, Part III* (Harvard University, 1977, typewritten). Criterion Judgment #6, Law Issue.
8. *Ibid.*, Criterion Judgment #5, Life Issue.
9. James Rest, "New Approaches in the Assessment of Moral Judgment," in Thomas Lickona, ed., *Moral Development and Behavior* (New York: Holt, Rinehart and Winston, 1976), p. 204.
10. Three good general sources are:
   —Lickona, ed., *Moral Development and Behavior*, chapter 1.

—Thomas C. Hennessy, S.J., ed., *Values and Moral Development* (Paramus, N.J.: Paulist/Newman Press, 1976).

—Peter Scharf, ed., *Readings in Moral Education* (Minneapolis, Minn.: Winston Press, 1978).

11. Jim Fowler, "Life/Faith Patterns" in Jim Fowler and Sam Keen, *Life Maps: Conversations on the Journey of Faith*, ed., Jerome Berryman (Waco, Tx.: Word Books, 1978).

CHAPTER V

1. Piaget, *Six Studies*, p. 63.
2. Joe W. McKinnon and John W. Renner, "Are Colleges Concerned with Intellectual Development?" *American Journal of Physics*, 39 (1971), 1047-52. These results are based on responses to tasks given 131 members of the freshman class at an Oklahoma university in which students had to think logically about problems of volume conservation, reciprocal implication of two factors, the elimination of a contradiction, the separation of several variables, and the exclusion of irrelevant variables from those relevant to problem solutions.
3. Lawrence Kohlberg and Carol Gilligan, "The Adolescent as a Philosopher: The Discovery of the Self in a Post-Conventional World," *Daedalus*, 100 (Fall 1971), 1065.

   This article also appears in Jerome Kagan and Robert Coles, eds., *Twelve to Sixteen: Early Adolescence* (New York: W. W. Norton, [1971], 1972), pp. 144-79. The results reported in this article are based on responses to the task of isolation of several variables. The other task presented was a correlation problem, passed by even fewer adults.
4. Pulaski, *Understanding Piaget*, pp. 66-76. This experiment was originally described in the following book dealing with formal operations:

   —Bärbel Inhelder and Jean Piaget, *The Growth of Logical Thinking from Childhood to Adolescence* (Basic Books, 1958), p. 108.
5. *Ibid.*, xx. Anne Parsons, "Translators' Introduction: A Guide for Psychologists."
6. Fowler, "Life/Faith Patterns."
7. Robert L. Oram.
8. Fowler, "Life/Faith Patterns," p. 89.
9. "Unitary Knowing—Intellectual Stage Beyond Science?" *Brain/Mind Bulletin*, 3 (October 2, 1978), 1.
10. William G. Perry, *Forms of Intellectual and Ethical Development in the College Years—A Scheme* (New York: Holt, Rinehart and Winston, [1968], 1970).
11. Piaget and Inhelder, *Psychology of the Child*, p. 149.
12. See note #8 for chapter 2.
13. *The New English Bible*, (Oxford and Cambridge University Press, 1970), Matthew 7:12.
14. Lawrence Kohlberg, "The Claim to Moral Adequacy of a Highest

Notes

Stage of Moral Judgment," *The Journal of Philosophy* 70, (Oct. 25, 1973), 642.

15. Joseph Chilton Pearce, *The Crack in the Cosmic Egg: Challenging Constructs of Mind and Reality* (New York: Julian Press, 1971), p. 57.
16. William Calley (with John Sack), *Lieutenant Calley: His Own Story* (New York: Viking Press, 1971). Quoted in Kohlberg and Scharf, "Bureaucratic Violence," p. 7.

CHAPTER VI

1. Lawrence Kohlberg, "From Is to Ought: How to Commit the Naturalistic Fallacy and Get Away with It in the Study of Moral Development," *Cognitive Development and Epistemology* (New York: Academic Press, 1971), p. 199.
2. Egil Krogh, statement, quoted in Candee, "Moral Psychology of Watergate," p. 186.
3. Lawrence Kohlberg, *Form A—Standard Scoring Manual*, Harvard University, Jan. 30, 1973, p. 23.
4. Carolyn Swearingen, "Dialogues on Hoping," *Strategy Magazine*, December 1975–February 1976, 5.

CHAPTER VII

1. Fowler, "Life/Faith Patterns," p. 81.
2. *Ibid.*, p. 89.
3. Kohlberg and Gilligan, "Adolescent as Philosopher," p. 1075.
4. Robert G. Kegan, "Constructions of Community," 51 ff. This paper by Kegan of Harvard University was presented in an earlier form to the 1973 Fall Conference of the Society for the Scientific Study of Religion, in San Francisco. It has made significant contributions to my understanding of social perspective, especially of Stage 4½ and Stage 6, and of transitions between stages.
5. *Ibid.*, p. 57.
6. *Ibid.*, p. 60.
7. James W. Fowler, "Stages in Faith: The Structural-Developmental Approach," in Hennessy, ed., *Values and Moral Development*, p. 200.
8. Lawrence Kohlberg, "Moral Stages and Moralization," in Lickona, ed., *Moral Development and Behavior*, p. 35.
9. Dan Candee, "Moral Psychology of Watergate," pp. 185-86.
10. *Ibid.*, p. 187.
11. *Ibid.*, p. 192.
12. Fowler, "Life/Faith Patterns," p. 82.

CHAPTER VIII

1. Kohlberg, "Moral Stages and Moralization," p. 35.
2. Kohlberg, *et al.*, *Assessing Moral Stages*.

3. Kegan, "Constructions of Community," p. 66.
4. Fowler, "Stages in Faith," p. 202.
5. Kohlberg, "From Is to Ought," p. 210.
6. Kohlberg, "Claim to Moral Adequacy," pp. 632-33.
7. *Ibid.*, p. 643.
8. *Ibid.*
9. *Ibid.*, p. 644.
10. Fowler, "Life/Faith Patterns," p. 90.

CHAPTER IX

1. Lickona, *Moral Development and Behavior*, p. 5, quoting from Lawrence Kohlberg, "The Relations Between Moral Judgment and Moral Action: A Developmental View." (Paper presented at Institute of Human Development, University of California at Berkeley, March 1969).
2. Kohlberg, *Assessing Moral Stages, Part III*, Table of Contents for "Issue of Contract," pp. 1-5.
3. Kohlberg, "Moral Stages and Moralization," p. 41.
4. Jane Loevinger, *Ego Development* (San Francisco: Jossey-Bass, 1976), pp. 133-34.
5. Kohlberg, *et al.*, *Assessing Moral Stages, Part I*, p. 33.
6. Lawrence Kohlberg, "Stage and Sequence: The Cognitive-Developmental Approach to Socialization," in David A. Goslin, ed., *Handbook of Socialization Theory and Research* (Chicago: Rand McNally, 1969), p. 395.
7. Richard Krebs and Lawrence Kohlberg, "Moral Judgment and Ego Controls as Determinants of Resistance to Cheating," in Lawrence Kohlberg and E. Turiel, eds., *Recent Research in Moral Development*, New York: Holt, Rinehart and Winston, forthcoming.
8. Kohlberg, "Stage and Sequence," p. 392.
9. Dan Candee, "Moral Psychology of Watergate," p. 191.
10. Thomas Lickona, "Critical Issues in the Study of Moral Development and Behavior," in Lickona, ed., *Moral Development and Behavior*, p. 17.
11. Kohlberg, "Stage and Sequence," p. 397.
12. Some of the ideas for the decision-making procedure are described in excellent detail in Lawrence E. Metcalf, ed., *Values Education: Rationale, Strategies and Procedures* (National Council for the Social Studies, 1201 Sixteenth St., N.W., Washington, D.C. 20036), 1971.

CHAPTER X

1. H. Hartshorne and M. A. May, *Studies in the Nature of Character: I Studies in Deceit; II Studies in Self-Control; III Studies in the Organization of Character* (New York: Macmillan, 1928-30).
2. Lawrence Kohlberg, "Stages of Moral Development as a Basis for Moral Education," in C. M. Beck, B. S. Crittenden, and E. V.

Notes

Sullivan, eds., *Moral Education* (Toronto: University of Toronto Press, 1971), pp. 75, 77.

3. *Ibid.*, p. 77.
4. Richard M. Jones, *Fantasy and Feeling in Education* (New York: New York University Press, 1968). This book is a ground-breaker in the area of coordination of cognitive, emotional, and imaginal approaches to education.
5. Important publications in this field are:
   —Robert E. Ornstein, *The Psychology of Consciousness* (New York: Viking Press, 1972).
   —Thomas Roberts and Frances Clark, *Transpersonal Psychology in Education* (Bloomington, Indiana: The Phi Delta Kappa Educational Foundation, 1975). An excellent small pamphlet, can be ordered from Phi Delta Kappa, Eighth and Union, Box 789, Bloomington, Ind. 47401.
   —Bob Samples, *The Metaphoric Mind* (Reading, Mass.: Addison-Wesley, 1976).
6. Sources for information on the enactive mode can be found in the following:
   —Jerome Bruner, *Toward a Theory of Instruction* (New York: W. W. Norton, 1966), p. 10.
   —Jerome S. Bruner, Rose R. Olver, Patricia M. Greenfield, *et al.*, *Studies in Cognitive Growth* (New York: Wiley, 1966), chapter 10. A detailed presentation of research in the use of three modes of learning and of the place of the enactive.
7. *Ibid.*, p. 220.
8. Barbara J. Katz, "How Kids Use What They Learn," *National Observer* (March or April issue, 1977), p. 6.
9. I first encountered the term "confluent education" defined by George Isaac Brown as "the term for the integration or flowing together of the *affective* and *cognitive* elements in individual and group learning—sometimes called humanistic or psychological education." George Isaac Brown, *Human Teaching for Human Learning* (New York: Viking Press, 1971), p. 3.
10. Moshe M. Blatt and Lawrence Kohlberg, "Effects of Classroom Moral Discussion upon Children's Level of Moral Judgment," in Kohlberg and Turiel, eds., *Recent Research in Moral Development*.
11. *Ibid.*, pp. 10-11.
12. Maureen Joy, "Reaction to Kavanagh: Observations on Methodology, Males and Religious Schooling," in Hennessy, ed., *Values and Moral Development*, p. 140.
13. Kohlberg, "Cognitive-Developmental Approach to Moral Education," p. 676.
14. Elsa R. Wasserman, "Implementing Kohlberg's 'Just Community Concept' in an Alternative High School," *Social Education*, 40 (April 1976), 203-7. Also found in Scharf, ed., *Readings in Moral Education*, pp. 164-73. See also pp. 137-95.
15. Marion Ostruske, *Educators' Guide to Media and Methods*, 5 (April 1969), bottom line of pages 44-53.
16. Decision-making and educational models have been worked out over a number of years through my experiences with many persons.

I particularly want to acknowledge the contributions to my own thinking of Orville E. Chadsey, H. Edward Everding, Clarence H. Snelling, and Dana W. Wilbanks.

Some articles by Kohlberg emphasizing education are:

—"Education for Justice: A Modern Statement of the Platonic View," in N. Sizer and T. Sizer, eds., *Moral Education* (Cambridge: Harvard University Press, 1970).

—"A Cognitive-Developmental Approach to Moral Education," *The Humanist* (November/December 1972).

—"The Moral Atmosphere of the School," in N. Overley, ed., *The Unstudied Curriculum*, Monograph of the Association for Supervision and Curriculum Development, Washington, D.C., 1970.

—L. Kohlberg and R. Mayer, "Development as the Aim of Education," *Harvard Educational Review*, 42 (November 1972).

—Scharf, ed., *Readings in Moral Education*, pp. 196-247.

CHAPTER XI

1. Barry K. Beyer, "Conducting Moral Discussions in the Classroom" in Scharf, ed., *Readings in Moral Education*, pp. 64-65.

2. For a start, here are some useful materials I've tried:

   —Beverly A. Mattox, *Getting It Together: Dilemmas for the Classroom Based on Kohlberg's Approach* (San Diego: Pennant Press, 1975). A collection of dilemmas for students from first grade through high school. The quality of the dilemmas varies in their usefulness for moral reasoning, but this is a helpful resource.

   —Moshe Blatt, Anne Colby, and Betsy Speicher, *Hypothetical Dilemmas for Use in Classroom Moral Discussions* (Cambridge: Harvard University Press, Moral Education Research Foundation, 1974). An extensive collection of moral dilemmas dealing with a wide variety of subjects. For high school age and adults.

   —*First Things: Values*, (Pleasantville, New York: Guidance Associates, 1972). Six sets of filmstrips, developed in consultation with Lawrence Kohlberg and Robert Selman, presenting moral dilemmas. Each set includes filmstrips, records or cassettes, and a discussion guide. Generally of good quality although we have encountered a few problems. Discussion guides are very helpful. The set, "What Do You Do About Rules?" has been especially popular. Prepared for elementary school, but some have been used successfully with junior-highs.

   —An additional reference that has received favorable comment, directed toward parents or teachers of very young children is Larry C. Jenson, *That's Not Fair! Helping Children Make Moral Decisions* (Provo, Utah: Brigham University Press, 1977).

3. Beyer, "Conducting Moral Discussions," p. 66.

4. Sidney B. Simon, Leland W. Howe, and Howard Kirschenbaum, *Values Clarification* (New York: Hart, 1972), p. 20.

5. *Ibid.*, p. 116.

6. *Ibid.*, p. 38.

7. *Ibid.*, p. 58.

Notes

8. Erik H. Erikson, *Identity, Youth and Crisis* (New York: W. W. Norton, 1968).
9. Norris M. Sanders, *Classroom Questions: What Kinds?* (New York: Harper, 1966). Another excellent source is Arthur A. Carin and Robert B. Sund, *Developing Questioning Techniques: A Self-Concept Approach* (Columbus, Ohio: Charles E. Merrill, 1971). Includes both affective and cognitive domains, many helpful examples.

CHAPTER XII

1. Fowler, "Stages in Faith," pp. 175, 179.
2. Everding and Wilcox, "Implications of Kohlberg's Theory for Biblical Interpretation."
3. *Good News for Modern Man* (New York: American Bible Society, 1966), Matthew 7:12.
4. Suggested in its original form by Dr. Clarence H. Snelling, Professor of Teaching Ministries, Iliff School of Theology.
5. *Good News.*
6. *The Lost Son* (New York: American Bible Society, 1966, 1971), Luke 15:11-32.
7. John Dominic Crossan describes one role of parables as the overturning of the assumptions, expectations, and security of our accustomed world-view. He does not relate this to a developmental frame of reference, but in raising these developmental questions, the correlations often appear to be very clear. Two of Crossan's books that are relevant to this study are:
   —*In Parables* (New York: Harper, 1973).
   —*The Dark Interval: Towards a Theology of Story* (Niles, Ill.: Argus Communications, 1975). This second book not only treats the subject of the reversal of expectations created by parables, but explores the function of story (myth) in the creation of one's world.
8. Erikson, *Identity, Youth and Crisis.*
9. Ronald Goldman, *Religious Thinking from Childhood to Adolescence* (New York: Seabury Press, 1968).
10. Ronald Goldman, *Readiness for Religion* (New York: Seabury Press, 1970, 1971), pp. 138, 17.
11. Information available through Morehouse-Barlow Co., 14 East 41st St., New York, N.Y. 10017.
12. This grid was prepared wih Gary Whetstone, student teaching intern.
13. *Holy Bible*, Revised Standard Version (Camden, N.J.: Thomas Nelson, 1952), I Corinthians 13:12.
14. Roland S. Larson and Doris E. Larson, *Values and Faith* (Minneapolis, Minn.: Winston Press, 1976).
   —Robert Meyners and Claire Wooster, *Solomon's Sword: Clarifying Values in the Church* (Nashville: Abingdon, 1977). This book has a variety of techniques and relates them to diversity within the church and to the church's concern with social issues.
15. An excellent book directed toward relating moral reasoning to the church is Ronald Duska and Mariellen Whelan, *Moral Develop-*

ment: *A Guide to Piaget and Kohlberg* (Paramus, N.J.: Paulist/ Newman Press, 1975).

16. John H. Westerhoff has written extensively on the role of the church as community in the development of faith. I particularly recommend two of his books that have been significant to my own thinking:
    —John H. Westerhoff, *Will Our Children Have Faith?* (New York: Seabury Press, 1976).
    —John H. Westerhoff and Gwen Kennedy Neville, *Generation to Generation* (Philadelphia: United Church Press, 1974).

17. Jack Renard Pressau, *I'm Saved, You're Saved . . . Maybe* (Atlanta: John Knox Press, 1977), pp. 44, 50-56.

18. From research now in progress. Title of project: "Developing a Theory of Instruction for Theological Education," being conducted by Mary M. Wilcox, Clarence H. Snelling, and H. Edward Everding. This project is supported by The Association of Theological Schools, The Andrew W. Mellon Foundation, The Arthur Vining Davis Foundation, and The Iliff School of Theology.

19. Idries Shah, *The Way of the Sufi* (New York: Dutton, 1970), pp. 204, 205.

INDEX

Index